SCHOOLCRAFT COLLEGE LIBRARY

W9-BLV-854

BX
4705
.S612
N63

Noonan, Daniel
The passion of
Fulton Sheen
WITHDRAWN

BX
4705
.S612
N63

Noonan, Daniel
The passion of
Fulton Sheen

BRADNER LIBRARY.
SCHOOLCRAFT COLLEGE
LIVONIA, MICHIGAN 48152

THE PASSION OF FULTON SHEEN

THE
PASSION
OF
FULTON SHEEN

BY

The Reverend D. P. Noonan

ILLUSTRATED WITH PHOTOGRAPHS

DODD, MEAD & COMPANY

NEW YORK

BX
4705
.S612
N63

Acknowledgment is gratefully made to the following for the use of material: Morris L. West and P. R. Reynolds and Co. for quotations from the play *The Heretic*; *The Reader's Digest* for quotation from the article "A Few Friends" by John Reddy; the Liveright Corporation and A. S. Barnes and Co. for quotations of Louis Nizer; McGraw Hill, Inc. for quotations from *The Priest Is Not His Own, The Life of Christ,* and *The World's First Love,* by Fulton J. Sheen; Bernadette Devlin and Pan Books for quotations from *Price of My Soul*; Harper & Row for quotation from *Profiles in Courage* by John F. Kennedy; Charles McKay for quotation of the poem "I Have a Rendezvous With Death" by Alan Seeger. Thanks are also due to William F. Buckley, Jr., Mike Wallace, David Frost, and Mike Douglas for permission to quote from interviews by them with Archbishop Sheen. Among newspapers and magazines used as source material were *The New York Times,* to which permission is acknowledged for the quotations in the chapters "Peace of Mind and Peace of Soul," the *Herald-Tribune, New York Post* and *Time.*

282.092
S539n

Copyright © 1972 by The Reverend D. P. Noonan

All rights reserved

No part of this book may be reproduced in any form without permission in writing from the publisher

ISBN: 0-396-06438-8
Library of Congress Catalog Card Number: 70-173885

PRINTED IN THE UNITED STATES OF AMERICA
BY THE CORNWALL PRESS, INC., CORNWALL, N. Y.

CONTENTS

ILLUSTRATIONS

Following page 88

THE MAN AND THE MYTH

THE RADIO CLOCK alarm awoke me suddenly but gently from a deep sleep. "This is the CBS News in New York, the 6 A.M. report." Here I was in San Francisco, the most beautiful city in the world. I arose promptly to prepare myself for the 6:30 A.M. mass at St. Brigid's Church, a wealthy parish, perched on Pacific Heights in the city by the Golden Gate. The day, October 28, 1966, was like any other day. Suddenly my ear became attuned to a terse news item: "His Holiness Pope Paul VI has appointed Fulton J. Sheen as Bishop of Rochester in upstate New York." My mind spontaneously went back to my seminary days, when I first knew of Sheen's existence through his writings and was deeply moved by them. I immediately recalled, too, how much influence he had had in the direction of my life.

At the early age of fourteen I became stricken in Ireland with a disease that was unmentionable at that time, T.B. I remember the year I spent on the flat of my back, the complete rest, and the good food, then the only well-known cures. I recollect, too, Eugene O'Neill's play, *Long Day's Journey into Night*, and how my own parents, like the principals in that drama, would admit anything but the fact that I had T.B. Apparently it was a social stigma, especially with the lace-curtain Irish.

My lungs surprisingly and suddenly healed. The river of time flowed on. I entered a missionary society to prepare for the missionary priesthood. I always doubted that I had the health for such a rigorous life, but my doubts were always settled by the facile remark, "It's the will of God." Ordained to the priesthood in 1958, I was in New York City in 1959 on my way to the waterfront of Buenos Aires, in the distant Argentine, to take up an appointment as an assistant dock chaplain.

Concern about my health being able to stand the ordeals of that demanding position began to trouble my mind. I wrote about my doubts to Fulton J. Sheen, at the address made nationally known my him—366 Fifth Avenue, New York City. A letter promptly came back, signed by him, suggesting I contact his personal secretary, Edith Brownett, about an appointment.

As I dressed for mass in that quiet San Francisco dawn, I remembered how excited I had been in keeping the appointment with the best-known churchman in the world. I recalled having nervously taken the elevator to the second floor, where I was welcomed by a receptionist who invited me to be seated. Within a few minutes Edith Brownett, a tall, striking blond, escorted me into the presence of the charismatic and photogenic churchman—a celebrity in his own right.

I was, at first, overawed. The air was full of electricity. Here I was in the presence of the prima donna of the American Church—the bishop with all the aura and mystique of a big Hollywood star. I told him my problem. For fifteen minutes he gave me a dramatic spiritual discourse, told me it was God's will that I go to Buenos Aires, gave me an autographed copy of one of his books, extended his ring to me to kiss, looked with his piercing eyes into mine, and said, "Bye now, and God love you."

I left his presence star struck. But when I had come out into the cool reality of a brisk New York autumn day, I suddenly realized he never addressed himself to my problem. And there, on New York's Fifth Avenue, I began to question, for the first time, who and what manner of man was this world-famous Fulton J. Sheen. But who was I, a simple priest, to doubt the motives of a bishop? And never ever if he were a Fulton Sheen.

As I dressed for mass, that tranquil October morn, I remembered, too, how Joe DiMaggio used to attend the 6:30 mass at St. Brigid's every Sunday morning, and what close friends we had become. I vividly recalled how the Yankee Clipper told me his impression of Sheen. Joe was married first in the Church, but when the marriage failed, he endeavored to obtain a church annulment in order to marry Marilyn Monroe, whom he deeply loved.

Sol Rosenblatt, the New York attorney who was the lawyer for both Sheen and Joe, suggested that Joe approach the former with his problem. Sheen dramatically told Joe, "If you had come to me before your first marriage, I would have told you never to have entered into it." It was like a doctor telling a patient who had broken his leg skiing and had gone to him to have it taken care of, "If you had come to me first, before you went on that ski weekend, I would have told you never to have gone." I recalled, too, the Yankee Clipper telling of his disappointment with Sheen, and that he had left his office immediately in utter disgust.

On the other hand, Sheen has attracted all types of people to himself from all walks of life. I remember, when I worked with Sheen, Paul Scott coming to visit him at least twice. Paul, an eighteen-year-old student with a shock of auburn hair, was a popular member of the senior class at a suburban New York high school. He suddenly developed symptoms similar to those of polio. His parents, thoroughly alarmed, took him to New York's Hospital for Joint Diseases. A woman doctor finally made the diagnosis. "I'm afraid, Paul," she said, "you have leprosy." With those few words, the carefree world of Paul Scott collapsed. It couldn't be, the boy thought; leprosy was something that happened in Asia or Africa, not in New York and not to him. Yet, it was true. The disease spread rapidly and ravaged his whole body. Just as his condition was becoming desperate, doctors discovered Sulphone, the drug that cures leprosy. After six tortured years, he was discharged from the hospital. However, the disease left its mark. He was crippled and disfigured. He avoided going out in public, but would wander along deserted beaches on weekends or around the empty streets of New York late at night, when few people were about.

One wet, blustery, Halloween night, he encountered under a street lamp a group of children in "trick or treat" costumes. Looking at him, one exclaimed, pointing at his disfigured face, "He doesn't need a mask." At these cruel words, spoken in childish innocence, Scott walked away blindly into the darkness, numb with rage and bitterness. All this hurt and humiliation welled up in fury and despair. Chance brought him to St. Patrick's Cathedral. Though not a Catholic, he went in. Kneeling there, he remembered he had heard of Bishop Sheen's great work for the lepers overseas. He went to see the Bishop.

"I have come to you, because I have no one else to turn to. I haven't a friend in the world."

"Well you have one now," said the Bishop. "You will never have many friends, but those you will have, will be true friends."

The first of these true friends was Bishop Sheen. He invited Paul once a week to dinner. Because it was difficult for Paul to use his hands, the Bishop cut the meat for him. He helped him find and furnish an apartment. Whenever the Bishop appeared on TV, he invited Paul to sit in the audience. Paul became a Catholic. Slowly his bitterness disappeared. Yet, at times, he suffered from loneliness.

"Friendship is like most things of value," the Bishop told him. "It is not easily found, but there is value even in loneliness. It will help you to appreciate the importance of friendship when it comes to you."

Paul did meet many true friends. He is alive again. He realizes his life will never be normal, but he has courage to face it. Friendships now seem as precious as rubies. The simplest acts of companionship—a date for lunch, an afternoon at the beach with a friend, an hour of conversation—these are moments to be cherished. Paul was one leper Sheen helped at home. He aided millions abroad.

I went to Buenos Aires. The humidity of the climate caused a reinfection of my lungs. Streptomycin and bed rest were prescribed. In 1960 the Archdiocese of Buenos Aires had a great mission—a religious crusade. The Church took to the streets for three weeks. Priests were imported from Spain, Italy, and the United States to participate. Sheen came to perform on television. My superior at that time was a former pupil of Sheen's. The Bishop came to visit him in our humble abode. That was the second time I saw Sheen. He came to my quarters where I lay ill, made some flowery remarks, autographed one of his books which I had in Spanish, and disappeared into the night.

I went back to Europe for another year to recuperate, then returned to the United States to work in a New York parish. That was the third time I met Sheen. He invited me to work for him as his special assistant. Thus, I began to know the man and the myth.

Sheen was born near Peoria, Illinois. He resigned from his last post at what some would call a clerical Siberia—Rochester, in upstate New York. In between he became probably the best-known bishop in the history of his Church. It is a long trek from Peoria to Rochester. This is the story of the controversial churchman who walked that painful road, and the convulsions of his Church and the world in the last seventy years, and his place in that Church and that world. He was touted as Spellman's successor in New York, and even a few unknowing, devout Catholic ladies thought he would be the first Yankee Pope. Many wonder why Sheen never became a cardinal and why he did not get a more prestigious position in the Church. This story will portray him, "warts and all," and will attempt to answer that question.

Was Sheen ahead of his time, and like all who seek to open up new frontiers, misunderstood? Or did he live out fully the roles of the Greek tragedy? Did he possess the Lyndon Johnson syndrome—hubris, a wanton arrogance? Was Rochester his calvary—a nemesis? Or in the final analysis, did he carry within himself the seeds of self-destruction—the fate leading to clerical hara-kiri? All his life this intriguing individual has been a sign of contradiction. This is the story of the enigmatic man from Peoria.

CHAPTER

1

THE MAN FROM PEORIA

THE GREAT voice of Fulton John Sheen was heard for the first time on May 8, 1895, in the room above Newton Sheen's hardware store in the little-known Illinois town of El Paso. Even then he had a wonderful voice, which caused one of his uncles to remark, "You could hear him crying for three blocks."

When Sheen was very young, the family moved to Peoria, about thirty miles away, where his father spent his time between storekeeping and farming. The infant had been baptized Peter John and was called "P.J." during his boyhood. Much of his early youth he spent with his grandparents, the Fultons, and he used the name Fulton until it stuck. It has been claimed that he was spoiled by his grandparents; during that period he became a loner, and so the seeds of his later withdrawal from the role of the common man were sown.

Sheen's father was a Catholic who for a time had drifted away from the fold, but had come back. So Sheen grew up in a home where evening prayers were the order of the day. He always insists there never was a time when he wanted to be anything but a priest. He went the usual route, attending Catholic schools, serving as an altar boy. He received an early start in the practical side of religion when he solicited advertising for the Church paper, *The Cathedral Messenger*.

Sheen went to St. Viator's College, Bourbonnais, Illinois. He was an excellent student who was not given to sports, although in later life he became a great devotee of tennis. He was involved in the undergraduate program and was a frequent contributor to the college magazine. At this early stage of his life, his great writing ability was emerging, to be attested to later by the publication of seventy books and countless magazine articles. Although he was not much interested in girls at that time, former classmates remember, in particular, a chic little French girl whom he used to see. Legend has it she later became a nun. Even in those early days the myth and the reality were beginning. Sheen decided he had a vocation in the priesthood, and so he went to St. Paul's Seminary in Minnesota to begin the long road to ordination. Nothing eventful occurred during his arduous apprenticeship—prayer, penance, long hours of study, and rigorous discipline were the order of the day. Sheen was raised to the priesthood in 1919 in an America just recovering from a terrible World War. He would later recount that on his ordination day he reached the pinnacle of happiness. Unlike the average newly ordained priest, who usually is assigned to a parish, Sheen, because of his great intellectual prowess, was sent to the Catholic University of America in Washington, D.C., to do graduate work.

In Washington, Sheen made his debut as a preacher. (In his time he was to become one of the world's great preachers.) The regular visiting priest at a certain Washington Church, who was scheduled to preach one Sunday, had to leave town because of a family illness. He asked Sheen to substitute for him. Sheen showed up at the rectory just five minutes before the beginning of mass. The pastor said to him in a gruff voice, "Get over to the Church. The other altar boys are dressed already." Sheen was a great hit, and like the man who came to dinner, he stayed and stayed, and preached and preached. And so began a brilliant and unique career.

Sheen then went to Europe with his brother Tom (presently a Manhattan physician) to study at the University of Louvain, Belgium. In the twenties, as again now, Louvain was a fashionable college for a priest's postgraduate work. To learn French, the brothers Sheen—Fulton and Tom—went to a small resort where no one spoke English. Soon after arriving, Fulton met a French woman who lived on the floor above them. Because of family trouble she was on the verge of despair and contemplating suicide. Sheen begged her to hold off for nine days. She agreed, and for eight evenings straight, Sheen discussed religion with her— "discussed," never argued. His motto always has been "Win an argument, and lose a soul." His French was so poor he kept a dictionary constantly open before him. On the ninth day, the woman entered the Church. Thus, Sheen had his first convert, the first of many well known later on—also of many, not well known.

Thus began some of the happiest years of Sheen's life. He was a wonderful student and possessed great stamina for studying. He was lucky in this—there was little else one could do in Louvain. All the classes were conducted in Latin and French; the professors were the most learned men in Europe of their time.

In 1923 Father Sheen obtained his Doctorate in Philosophy from Louvain. He was then invited to take another degree, a super Ph.D. called Agrégé en Philosophie, an invitation which only about ten students had received over a period of forty years. To obtain this degree, Father Sheen worked for two years, part of the time in Rome, and part in England. One of the requirements for the degree was fulfilled by a book, *God and Intelligence*, which many claim to be his finest.

A day was set for his final examination. During his stay in Louvain Father Sheen was very generous to a destitute family. Although at times he thought they were taking advantage of him, he continued to help them. Very early on the morning of his final test, he saw all the family trudging down the street. They told him they had gone to the Shrine of Our Lady of Montaigne, a distance of twenty-five miles from Louvain. There they had spent the night in prayer for his success.

The public examination took place before about three hundred people—professors from countries throughout Europe. All were present to question the candidate. The examination lasted from 9 A.M. until late in the afternoon. Father Sheen then went to his quarters. If someone knocked at his door and invited him to dinner with the professors, that was the sign he was successful. The beverages served would be the indication of the degree of his success. If he passed with satisfaction, water would be served; with great distinction, wine; with the highest distinction—well, that evening the lights in Louvain had been on for a half hour when Father Sheen received the invitation to dinner. As he entered the dining room, the waiters began to serve champagne.

Sheen has recounted the following incident many times publicly and also in my presence. While he was in Europe, the fifth anniversary of his priesthood approached. Sheen decided to visit Lourdes to celebrate the occasion. He had just the train fare to Lourdes. His brother Tom was broke too. Sheen said to himself, "If I have enough faith to go to Lourdes to celebrate my fifth anniversary, the Blessed Mother will take care of me." He arrived in Lourdes penniless and registered at the best hotel in town. He made a novena, nine days of prayer looking for help. After nine days, he received his hotel bill; it was beyond his wildest imaginings. He had visions of being arrested by the French police. On the evening of the ninth day, he went to the Grotto of Our Lady of Lourdes "to give her a last chance."

A tall gentleman tapped him on the shoulder and said, "Are you an American priest? I'm from New York. Do you speak French? Yes? Would you come to Paris and act as our interpreter? Have you paid your hotel bill yet?" Naturally, Sheen did not outreach him for the check. At this early stage Sheen was exhibiting his penchant for drama.

Also while studying in Europe, Sheen did parish work in a poor neighborhood, St. Patrick's, Soho, a section of the city of London not far from Piccadilly Circus. Thus began his contact with the poor. The parish was half Italian and half London Irish, with a sprinkling of Chinese. Everytime he goes to London, he still preaches there, where he remains a loved and legendary figure. One parishioner said of his visits, "Things seem very confused. Then you have a talk with Sheen. Then things clear up. Then they become confused again."

Sheen has told many times the following moving incident which took place during his stay in Soho. It was a dark winter's morn. As he opened the front door of the Church, he noticed a woman lying inside, apparently under the influence of drink. Father Sheen helped her to her feet and recognized her face. She was the star of a play on the West End of London. Her life, she said, was a mess—one affair after another, and now she was on the brink of ending it all. Father Sheen asked her to go home, pull herself together, and come back to talk to him. She promised to do this, provided he would not ask her to go to confession. She came back later in the day. Sheen showed her around the Church. As he was passing the confessional, he pushed her in. He did not ask her to go; he kept his promise. She made her peace with God and became a nun.

Sheen had received many academic distinctions and had tasted a little of parish life; now he faced a crisis such as confronts many a man sometime in his life—the conflict of his own will versus that of his superiors. At a moment of great personal triumph Sheen was being put to the test. The rector of the University of Louvain was a personal friend of Nicholas Murray Butler, the then president of Columbia University. The two men discussed the idea of Sheen's going to Columbia University as professor of Thomistic Philosophy. Cardinal Bourne of England wanted him to go to Oxford with Monsignor Ronald Knox to start a Catholic college there. Then came the moment of truth. Bishop Dunne of Peoria, Illinois, Sheen's ecclesiastical superior, summoned him home. In September 1925, in the seventh year of his priesthood, this brilliant Church scholar arrived back in the United States. He immediately received many more teaching offers. The one that appealed to him most came from Detroit, where Church officials wanted him to organize and head their philosophy department in the seminary. Sheen liked the offer. He wrote to Bishop Dunne, suggesting permission to accept it. Dunne's answer was simple—"No. God will provide."

Dunne assigned Sheen as assistant pastor to St. Patrick's Church in Peoria—a parish which thirty years previously was one of the best in the city, but now had deteriorated.

A monk in a monastery will tell you that the toughest thing about monastic life is not the pleasure one gives up, but the obedience. This is true of any priest or any human being. Sheen threw himself wholeheartedly into the endless routine of parish work—instructing the children in school, visiting the sick, burying the dead, baptizing, preaching. In the late summer of 1926 Father Sheen was informed that Dunne wanted to see him. The Bishop said, "You are going to the Catholic University in Washington, D.C., as a Professor of Philosophy." Father Sheen asked, "Why did you not send me on my return from Europe." The Bishop answered, "Because after the success you had in Europe, it was rumored you would obey nobody. I wanted to find out if you were obedient, and would do what you were told."

Was Bishop Dunne fair to Sheen in putting him to such a test, or did he at that early stage see in Sheen a wanton arrogance, the beginnings of the first act of the Greek tragedy? It has been said of Sheen that while he would like to be known as a popularist, he was at heart a king. And so the man from Peoria, Illinois, took the train to Washington, to more fame and fortune. Sheen was learning that no matter how dark the night, the dawn would come, or, as Albert Camus said, "In the midst of winter, I finally learned there was in me an invincible summer." And so in Washington, as professor at the Catholic University, Sheen began the summer of his years. The champagne served that night in Louvain in his hour of triumph was still bubbling; he was now doing what he would like best—he was going onward and upward. Had he found his true vocation at last as professor?

CHAPTER

2

THE PROFESSOR

THE CATHOLIC UNIVERSITY in Washington, D.C., is a pontifical university. It is governed strictly and financed by the American bishops. Soon again, Sheen was faced with a critical decision. His first book, *God and Intelligence*, his actual thesis in Louvain, was being very well received, and is even still regarded as a classic in Catholic circles. Father Sheen could have chosen as his goal classical philosophy leading to a quiet life, or he could follow his inclinations for the response of the crowds to his persuasive voice. He chose the latter.

Sheen became one of the best-known professors at Catholic University, and his fame grew. Washington hostesses considered him a prize catch. He moved into an expensive house designed to order for him, startlingly modernistic. For heavy work, he set up his workshop in the furnace room, piled high with books and papers. He was aloof from the students and was not involved in the campus life.

Sheen became a popular philosopher. There were those

who believed that had he remained a classical philosopher, he would have been the St. Thomas of the twentieth century. However, he needed the roar and approval of admiring audiences. He appeared on the first program of the "Catholic Hour" in 1930 and remained its shining star until he graced the TV screen. He never lacked invitations for sermons, communion breakfasts, rallies, and banquets. For years, until he crossed words with Cardinal Spellman, he preached a Lenten series in New York's famous St. Patrick's Cathedral. He became the popular choice, the outstanding orator and apologist for the Catholic Church in America. Thousands who heard him on radio sought him out for personal guidance and counsel. He remained on the faculty of Catholic University for twenty-five years, but his duties for much of this period were minimal. His classes, however, were very popular, and many audited them. He was an exciting professor with a beautiful delivery and crystal clear explanation. He was not, however, friendly with the students. He believed in monologue, not dialogue.

Sheen had just a simple graduate course a year. Father Ignatius Smith, Sheen's boss in the philosophy department, said of him, "I was often criticized for not giving him more work, but I felt he was doing more good on the outside." Father Smith recalled once remonstrating with him for allowing no questions during his outside lectures. Sheen replied that his explanations were so clear there could not possibly be any questions. This was an arrogant remark from an incipient prima donna.

Sheen also had difficulties with the National Council of
Catholic Men who arranged the "Catholic Hour." He was
required to submit an advance manuscript, but he had the
habit of adlibbing and running overtime. Although they
scheduled five minutes for music, Sheen did not care for
music on the show, and he particularly disliked having his
time shared. He always loved center stage; he never, ever,
liked sharing the spotlight.

Sheen entertained a great deal at his splendid white-brick
house on Hawthorne Lane in Washington, with its spectacular white circling staircase and broad windows overlook-
ing a verdant view. It was a comfortable place, with two
studies, a private chapel, and piped-in music. In the evening
there was always impeccably arranged a drink or two before dinner, an excellent meal, and wonderful, varying talk,
dominated by Sheen. In 1934 Sheen became a monsignor.
I remember his once recounting how some United States
bishop wanted him to become his auxiliary bishop. Sheen
refused to have his name go to Rome. He quipped: "There
are two ways to advancement in the Church: a push from
below, a pull from above. I prefer the latter." Louis Nizer,
introducing Sheen once to an audience, said of him:

Extraordinary men often spring from ordinary parents. In
a democracy, distinguished leaders can seldom pattern their
activities upon the achievements of their forebearers. But I
believe men elect spiritual ancestors from whom they derive
inspiration. Thus, writers and painters are usually influenced
by some outstanding predecessor. This is likewise true in the

political realm. For example, I think that Winston Churchhill followed the great pathway of another Prime Minister, William Pitt. Pitt was also faced with a tyrant—Napoleon—who had conquered Europe and who stood poised to cross the English Channel to strike England down. England then too showed doggedness and high courage which confounded military experts. It was William Pitt who said: "England has saved herself by her energy; now she must save Europe by her example." Monsignor Sheen also has a spiritual ancestor, literally as well as symbolically. He is St. Thomas Aquinas. St. Thomas was a writer, lecturer, and the greatest scholastic philosopher his Church ever produced. Fulton J. Sheen is also a writer. He has written more than thirty books. He is a lecturer and through the modern instrumentality of radio, he addresses millions of people each week on the Sunday "Catholic Hour." Two million copies of his speeches have been distributed. He is the foremost religious and scholastic philosopher of his day and has for many years been a Professor of Philosophy at Catholic University in Washington, D.C.

I find a curious fact in his background. His uncle was a lawyer and a partner of the famous atheist Robert G. Ingersoll. I do not know whether it was his uncle who made the famous retort to Ingersoll on atheism, but I should like to attribute it to him. It is said that Ingersoll was in a museum one day with his friend and admired a painting of a sky studded with stars and in which a bright moon lit up a turbulent sea. Ingersoll was fascinated. "Who did it?" The gentleman next to him, who I hope was Bishop Sheen's uncle, replied: "Why, Bob, no one did it. It just happened."

I once heard Sheen remark that he deemed the twenty-five years spent at the Catholic University in Washington as wasted. Today the whole question of Catholic schools is being debated, whether they are divisive in an already divided nation or whether they are fiscally feasible. In 1950 the push from below came. Sheen was summoned to New York to head up the national office of the Society for the Propagation of the Faith, the Church's overseas mission. The man from Peoria, Illinois, was being groomed for higher things by the man from Boston, Massachusetts. Sheen came to New York City to work under the aegis of Francis Cardinal Spellman. A bright future was assured, a cardinal's hat was hovering in the clerical air, and a prestigious diocese or archdiocese was his for the asking if he played the clerical game. Peaceful years were ahead; maybe, however, the battle was only beginning.

CHAPTER

3

WAR AND PEACE

"I SPEAK of peace—they are ready for war." As we walk that road from Peoria to Rochester, the enigma that is Sheen gradually unfolds. In the Gaelic language, Fulton means "war" and Sheen means "peace." Here again, as in all else, I find Sheen an ambiguous man. His early preachings and teachings against communism comprise one of the major portions of his life. Many thought in those days he was overplaying the question of communism, about which, between 1930 and 1936, some people were thinking kindly. It had become bad manners to denounce Russia—to criticize communism was a sign of intolerance. Particularly when Russia sided with the allies against Hitler, it became less fashionable to condemn her.

At that time Sheen was one of the few voices raised against the Red Menace. He saw no difference between communism and nazism. Stalin persecuted the New Testament; Hitler the Old Testament. Sheen said the only difference between nazism, fascism, and communism was the difference between burglary and stealing.

He did not, however, agree with Senator Joseph McCarthy in his approach to communism. Sheen attacked the philosophies rather than the personalities. He had a deep knowledge of the tenets of communism. He read every line of Marx and Lenin. He became thoroughly acquainted with the Russian constitution and once said that the atheism of the Communist would be silly if there were no God. He would be like Don Quixote tilting with imaginary windmills. One day in 1936 a very well dressed, middle-aged man called on Sheen at the Catholic University in Washington. He gave him a copy of a book of which he was the author. The book started with these words, "From now on I dedicate myself to the cause of God and America." He said he wanted to travel with Sheen. He wished for twenty minutes before each lecture to give a firsthand account of the evils of communism. Sheen told him he would let him know in a few days. Sheen, immediately suspicious, phoned the FBI, giving a description of the man. He was told by them that he was a dangerous Soviet spy.

Many of Sheen's radio broadcasts in the thirties were monitored. Was Roosevelt endeavoring to muzzle Sheen?

After World War II the loyalty of some Americans was questioned. Sheen did not take sides. He never met the late Senator Joseph McCarthy, who was solidly backed by Spellman even when McCarthy fell from his demagogic power. Sheen was insistent that although people must hate communism, they must love the Communist. His thesis was that communism is to be hated as a doctor hates pneumonia in a sick child. But the Communist, the potential child of God, must be loved as a sick child is loved. Was not Paul in the early Church as great a persecutor as Hitler or Stalin. There must have been thousands of Christians who in thought hoped that God would send a thrombosis to Paul of Tarsus. Rome was the greatest persecutor of religion until Russia in modern times. But Rome became the center of Christianity. What is to prevent God from transfiguring Russia, so that from it one day will radiate a light to renew faith in the Church and give it to Asia?

Stalin—as a man—cannot be categorized. He did not fit into the ordinary categories of human behavior. He was larger than life, almost larger than death. The convulsions he inflicted on Russia had little to do with Marxist theory, of which he was surprisingly ignorant. He was an indescribable criminal, and utterly ruthless. He was outside the reservation of humanity. This small, pockmarked man, with the withered arm, black teeth, and yellow eyes, was the greatest tyrant of his time, if not, indeed, of all times. Sheen once devoted a whole telecast to an imaginary eulogy that could be delivered at Stalin's death. Stalin cooperated with him by dying two weeks later.

Communism and the Conscience of the West is one of Sheen's finest books. It deals with the philosophy of communism. It is an indictment of its tenets, but it is also a stern reminder of the shortcomings and evils of our Western civilization, out of which communism has grown. For most of his life he had been an ardent foe of communism. He saw it as a type of secular religion based on an erroneous view of man and a denial of God. His theme was: Modern Christians have truth, but no zeal; the Communists have zeal, but no truth. They have heat, but no light. We have the light, but no heat. They have passion but no ideals; we have ideals but no passion. Sheen urged that all men of good-will adopt the zeal, heat, and passion of the Communists.

In the hot summer of 1967, Sheen said he was convinced that if President Johnson withdrew all United States troops from South Vietnam, he would become the moral leader of the world. Sheen had urged the President to withdraw troops "for the sake of reconciliation." Sheen again had a first—the first time that a member of the Roman Catholic Hierarchy in the United States had taken such a dovish position on the war in Vietnam. Considerable speculation and controversy were aroused as to what lay behind the Bishop's unusual statement. Was it a publicity stunt? Was Sheen joining the New Left? These were valid questions in the light of the fact that he was a Commie baiter in the 30's.

President Johnson that summer had asked the churches to pray for racial harmony. Sheen, with his faculty for a neat turn of phrase, asked himself whether this reconciliation must be limited only to black and white, why not to all colors and countries. He acknowledged he had organized aid for the million refugees who fled to the South. What

would happen to those? "We must take a pyramid of questions," Sheen said. "The most important question is that the
biggest power in the world must not be for several years
fighting the smallest countries." He gave some reasons for
his view: a depleted public treasury; the loss of men; the
alienation of public opinion. "I do not see that it is the
question altogether of Vietnam Catholicism; but of the
war's stopping so that the people could find a solution
among themselves." Sheen observed. "I am not concerned
with military or political questions. I only know that in a
quarrel, the burden is always on the stronger man to quit
first. What is primarily important, is that the greatest power
in the world has to move out." This view of Sheen was
basically the same as Pope Paul's, but characteristically opposed to Spellman's. Pope Paul VI, in his dramatic speech
at the UN, said, "war—war, never again." Subsequently the
following interview with Mike Wallace on CBS "Sixty
Minutes" occurred.

Wallace: "Two years ago, Archbishop, you called upon
President Johnson to unilaterally withdraw the U.S. forces
from Vietnam. You were the first major American Catholic
to do so. Are you still committed to that view?"

Sheen: "Yes, I am. First, it is not a political action. It's
a moral action. If we are to be the moral leaders in the
world, we must give an example and be the most powerful
also. We must show our power by appreciating the weak.
So, I suggested that we withdraw for the sake of winning
the approval of the world, and, furthermore, this war is

costing too much. In Vietnam it costs a million dollars an hour—twenty-four million a day. If we kill twenty-four men a day (and sometimes that is all that is killed) that means a million dollars a man. So that, from a moral and an economic point of view, withdrawal from Vietnam is to be very much recommended."

Wallace: "Now?"

Sheen: "Now."

Wallace: "Immediately?"

Sheen: "Immediately."

A few weeks later Sheen watered down this view. He said he agreed with Nixon's Vietnamization program. Where does Sheen stand? Here, as on many other issues, his view seems to change with the mood of the times. On the occasion of an interview with David Frost, the Britisher recalled that Sheen was one of the first to speak out against the Vietnamese War.

Sheen: "Well, I did make a statement two years ago and the statement that I made two years ago is not applicable now. What I said two years ago was, I wished we would withdraw unilaterally in order to give a moral example to the world."

Frost then asked what his views now are.

Sheen said, "It must be remembered that President Nixon knows a thousand things about the international situation and the war in Vietnam which we do not know." Sheen called for trusting the President's statement that he will withdraw United States forces as rapidly as possible. He

said, "An offensive war is never justified." Yet Spellman
called the United States troops in Vietnam "Soldiers of
Christ." Sheen admitted that a defensive war may be necessary in defense of country and citizens, but "never—never—
an offensive war. I think we must begin to make wars
against war."

In a verbal duel with William Buckley, editor, political
connoisseur of words, and a dyed-in-the-wool conservative,
Sheen said on the TV program "Firing Line," "Just think.
If we spent the same amount of money that we are spend-
ing on armaments today, to help the world, how much
better the world would be." Sheen was acknowledging that
it should be a function of the Church "constantly to measure
society against the gospel; continually challenging institutions to be people-oriented, continuously building cathedrals
not of stone, but in the minds and hearts of men." Buckley's
reply to Sheen was, "I think we would be much worse off
because the barbarians would be in complete control then.
Do you think the people are better off in Russia because
we didn't resist them, even though we had the opportunity
to do so 20 years ago?"

Apparently, Buckley wants America to be the policeman
of the world. Sheen's view would be that we were better
off being the pantry of the world, feeding the hungry and
giving the homeless and illiterate opportunities to help
themselves?

During his trip to Vietnam at Christmas of 1966, the late
Cardinal Spellman said that the United States must fight

for total victory. A button appeared, saying "Draft Spellman." At that time, a Vatican source said Spellman was reflecting his own views and not those of the Pope. The Pope felt a negotiated peace, rather than a military victory by either side, was the way to end the war. He had made this clear in countless speeches. Spellman said, "Anything less than victory is inconceivable."

Some people go so far as to question whether Sheen's views of the war were the result of the feud he had running with Spellman. Was this a way of getting even with the Spellman clerical complex? Or had Sheen grown away from his earlier hawkist views and become more dovish? Or was he just an opportunist, becoming the den mother of the New Left, doing the in thing, and becoming, not a hawk or a dove—but a parrot?

In the sunset days of the Diem regime, Diem's brother, Archbishop Thuc, the then Bishop of Hue, and his sister, Madame Nhu, whose forked tongue blunted her mission, toured the United States to bolster their brother's position. Archbishop Thuc was politicking in Rome for Diem, and Pope Paul kicked him out. In a press conference, Thuc announced he was taking off for the United States to meet with Spellman and Sheen to plead with them to intercede with the State Department for his stumbling brother. Sheen's office got a phone call from "The Powerhouse" on Madison Avenue announcing that Spellman would not see Archbishop Thuc, as he was annoyed with him. He suggested that Sheen refrain from seeing him and keep a united front. Sheen had Thuc to lunch. I was present on this in-

teresting occasion. Why did Spellman not raise a finger to
help Diem when Spellman had contributed to getting him
into power?

A kind of Catholic mandarin, Diem was a rabid anti-
Communist. In 1933 he helped the French fight the Communists in a Vietnamese anticolonial revolt. He decided this
was a futile crusade, so he went into exile for seventeen
years. He came to the United States, where he received
a lot of backing in the liberal academic world. He also got
support from the Catholic hierarchy. His brother, Archbishop Thuc, arranged for Diem to stay in Maryknoll
seminaries in New Jersey and New York. This was Spellman's hunting ground. Diem was anti-Communist and a
Catholic, with a bishop for a brother. Diem had sufficient
calling cards for an audience with the Cardinal. So the
episcopal kingmaker and Vietnamese mandarin became
friends. Apparently in 1955 Spellman got in touch with
Joseph Kennedy, Sr., and through him arranged for Senator Mike Mansfield to persuade a dubious and wavering
Eisenhower to help Diem get into power. Spellman was
most influential with Eisenhower. Obviously, Spellman was
interested in setting up a Catholic power pocket in the
Far East. Why did he do nothing to keep Diem in power
when the writing was on the wall for him? Was he pres-
sured by the State Department because Diem was no longer
viable, or was he forced to save face for the Catholic Church
because Diem was embarrassing it by the Buddhist self-immolations? I think the people have a right to know the
answer to these questions.

Did Sheen change his views on communism, or did he take a dovish stand just to oppose Spellman? Did Sheen have inside information or was he just again deciphering the mood of the New Left and capitalizing on the publicity involved? I think Sheen really owes an explanation. Apparently, the Buddhists' protests and self-immolations were political maneuvers to undercut Diem. Someone called it Spellman's war.

Christianity and communism each claim the allegiance of a third of the world's population, and traditionally each has preached a way of salvation requiring the destruction of the other. Since Pope John there has been an opening to the Left. As a result, many Roman reactionaries dubbed Pope John "The Red Pope." Intellectuals of both sides have sought a common ground for dialogue. Sheen was the Vatican's man in the United States for this dialogue.

Cardinal Midszenty, the primate of Hungary, took the hard line. In 1955, as the Soviet tanks pushed ominously through the streets of Budapest, he had to run for his life. During the Hungarian uprising he enjoyed only four days of freedom. He sought political asylum in the American Legation and has remained there ever since. Apparently the Hungarian Communist Government, the United States State Department, and surprisingly enough the Vatican wish he would give up and go away. Even more intransigent is Poland's Cardinal Stefan Wyszynski. He has said about Pope John's *apertura a sinistro* that John never grasped the meaning of communism.

Was the release of Maryknoll's Bishop Walsh in July of 1970 from twelve years imprisonment in a Chinese prison an indication of their willingness to have dialogue with the Vatican? Sheen, referring to the plight of the Church in Chile, once said that the Roman persecutions in the early Church were primarily physical, the Communist persecutions are primarily psychological. The first attacked the body, the second attacks the mind. The Romans made "wet martyrs," the Communists made "dry martyrs."

Sheen's thesis has been that the institutional Church tends to be a ghetto religion, consisting of the lily-white bourgeois with a tendency to join the powerful and privileged, and to neglect the oppressed and the minorities. Latin America is a prime example of this. The Church's advocacy of social justice, which in practice it neglects, would have spawned Communism with or without Marx. Chile, for instance, was the first country to elect an avowed Marxist President, Dr. Allende. The Catholic Church has alienated a major portion of the youth of the country for its failure to take a stand on the question of peace in Vietnam.

Once somewhat of a Ronald Reagan of the clergy—handsome, articulate, and a splendid communicator—Sheen took the hard line approach on communism. Yet when he changed his position he never ever went as far as the radical discipleship of the shock troops of the Catholic New Left, the Church's most militant and prolific writers on pacifism and civil rights—the brothers Berrigan. The two most famous members of the Catonsville Nine—Philip, also a leader of the Harrisburg six, and the Holy Outlaw Daniel claimed they burned draft cards in the name of God, who is decency, humanity, and love, hoping by this action to make clear that napalm is immorally and illegally destroying human lives in Vietnam, alleging the Church in the United States had been silent about the war in Vietnam. They are now paying the cost of such radical discipleship. Some people agree with their position but not their tactics. They attempt in their own way to live the scandal of the gospel; maybe they are part of the Church of the future. Sheen backed Franco in the Spanish Civil War. The Spanish leader emerged victorious and rules Spain as a fascist dictator.

This chapter on communism points to the complex, controversial character of Sheen. He became a living legend in his time, but like all legends, part fact, part fiction. He is an elusive man, difficult to place in any particular slot. To use Freudianese, he is split in the ego—a confusing, confused man who has the whole gamut of emotions between pride and humility, inferiority and superiority, all taking place in his tempestuous, tortured soul that utterly devastated that inner peace and freedom he so desperately searched for all his life. It is difficult to draw a portrait of Fulton Sheen, a mercurial human being, a dreamer, impulsive in action and ambiguous in almost everything he did. He looked so hard for peace; he seemed always to be at war. Would the real Fulton Sheen ever stand up?

CHAPTER
4

"GIVING A DAMN
ABOUT THE POOR"

SOME PEOPLE are born with silver spoons in their mouths, others are born with collection plates in their hands; such a one is Fulton J. Sheen. As we follow that pilgrimage from Peoria to Rochester we see on November 1, 1950, his coming to New York City to take over as national director of the Society for the Propagation of the Faith—the Catholic Church's overseas mission fund. Thus began another phase of his interesting but puzzling career. He was on his way up.

Sheen used to tell the story of the Chicago gangster who died and went to Heaven to be judged. St. Peter had a day off, and like any good priest, was probably out playing golf. St. Paul was pinch-hitting for him. Paul asked the gangster if he had at any time done something good in life. The gangster said, "No, but now that you mention it, I gave a dime once to Bishop Sheen for the missions." St. Peter, in the meantime, came back and inquired what the gangster was doing there. Paul said, "He gave a dime once to Bishop Sheen for the missions." Peter said, "Give him his dime back and tell him to go to hell." Nobody could mesmerize anyone with his eyes as Sheen used to do when he talked about the poor overseas. He asked for dimes, but wrapped in dollar bills.

For sixteen years Sheen was the national director of the Society for the Propagation of the Faith, with about 130 offices in the Catholic dioceses throughout the United States. There are national directors in many countries of the world. The head office, naturally in Rome, was then presided over by the astute, bearded Armenian, Gregory Cardinal Agagianian, with whom Sheen was consistently clashing over policy issues.

In October of 1970 Pope Paul named Angelo Cardinal Rossi, Archbishop of Sao Paulo and Chairman of the Brazilian Bishops' Conference, chief of the Roman Catholic Church's missions throughout the world. Rossi, who is in his late fifties, succeeded the ailing Agagianian, who was mentioned as a possible candidate for the papacy in 1958 and again in 1963.

As the new head of the Sacred Congregation for the Evangelization of the Peoples, the Vatican mission's center, Rossi is the first Latin American prelate to administer in the Church's inner circle, the Curia. Rossi's appointment is another example of a promotion in order to remove the appointee. His new position snatched from the Brazilian Church a conservative, at a time when the more progressive wings of the episcopacy and clergy are in open conflict with the military regime over alleged police brutality, no political freedom, and dire poverty.

Many would have liked Sheen to head the Society for the Propagation of the Faith in the 1960's. Apparently he did not play his clerical cards right. The Congregation Rossi now commands is responsible for the work of 36,000 priests, 15,500 religious, 82,000 nuns. It operates 100,000 schools with a 10 million enrollment and administers also about 1,000 hospitals. Roman Catholics throughout the world annually contribute about $30 million for its operation on all continents.

For years Sheen has been talking about world poverty, about the two-thirds of the people of the world who go to bed hungry every night, about the 40 million people who die of starvation each year.

Years before the war on poverty came into being, Sheen was carrying on his battle against poverty in a thousand slums of our big cities and in capitals throughout the world. Sheen in that crusade was influenced by the writings of Lady Jackson, who is better known as the economist Barbara Ward. Her interest in poverty began when she married Sir Robert Jackson in 1950. He worked with the United Nations Relief and Rehabilitation Agency and was appointed to advise on India's economic problem. This was Barbara Ward's first real experience with the human suffering which lay behind the figures and graphs of the economic charts.

Up to 1950 until he came to New York City, Sheen lived in an ivory tower as far as poverty was concerned. His sumptuous quarters in a fashionable Washington neighborhood and the society in which he mixed were hardly the milieu of the poor. Meeting missionaries from foreign lands and traveling himself in the underprivileged areas brought him into direct contact with the naked, the starved, and the poor.

There are three hundred missionary societies in the Catholic Church. Some are large like the Jesuits, the White Fathers who have nineteen hundred missionaries in Africa alone, or the Maryknoll and the Columban Fathers, with about six hundred priests scattered over Japan, the Philippines, South America, Korea, Burma, and the Fiji Islands. Each mission group helps its own, so the Church has to have an organization which aids all of them, in all places, and in an equitable manner.

The Third World has been the "Cinderella" of the Church. The Church tends to become a ghetto, an exclusive club of middle-class respectability in league with the powers that be, far removed from the muck and mud of daily living. It has been all tied up in big buildings at home, giving financial scraps to the missions overseas. Sheen, with his indefatigable preaching and famed writing, has been for seventeen years a champion of the poor. The Church, the institution, has never really put itself on the line for the poor. The performance never matched the promise.

Sheen said of the Propagation of the Faith, "This really is

the greatest philanthropic charitable organization in the world. Not one of our 135,000 missionaries, doctors, nurses, teachers, or social workers receives a cent of salary. They all labor for the glory of God. Our aid is not to Catholics alone. We help maintain 55,000 schools in Asia, Oceania, and part of Latin America. We have 6,000 hospitals and dispensaries, more than 300 leper colonies, with about 50,000 living in the colonies, and 10,000,000 outpatients. We have 1,300 orphanages and 700 homes for the aged."

In his many junkets soliciting funds for the Propagation of the Faith, Sheen used numerous means of transportation —train, bus, automobile, or taxi. He preferred the airplane, as it was the quickest way of getting to his destination. On one trip by railroad, he spent eighteen straight hours in a sleeper and came to the conclusion that a man loses all resemblance to the image of God when he takes his trousers off in an upper berth. Sheen's experience was that it is the poor who support the missions, not the rich. "Is it," he said, "because the money goes to the other parts of the world, or because when they give at home, they can see their names on libraries and in gymnasiums? But they cannot see their names in a leper colony—nor can they be thanked by the poor in India, nor by the victims of communism in Korea and Vietnam."

Mission is a catchy, bimonthly magazine founded by Sheen, which depicts the needs of the missions. Its multimillion circulation brought the dire necessity, the grinding poverty, the dehumanizing squalor of the Third World into millions of American homes. It was edited by Sheen himself. Some thought that he personalized it too much, referring to the castoffs of our society as Bishop Sheen's poor. However, he did accomplish the Trojan work of bringing the plight of the two-thirds of the world who are hungry to the attention of an era which was growing cynical and impersonal. Sheen's thesis was that the great schism of the twentieth century is the divorce between the haves and the have-nots. The 30th parallel is the geographical cutoff between them. Above the parallel are prosperous lands. Below are South America, Oceania, half of China and Africa, where most people live and die on garbage heaps.

Another mission magazine Sheen edited was *World Mission*, a scholarly work with a circulation of about five thousand. He also had a weekly syndicated column in all the Catholic papers of the country, soliciting aid for the needy overseas. It was called "God Loves You."

Was Sheen really committed to the poor? Was it his need for a crusade, or did he really have the compassion to be their spokesman? His life up to the time of his taking over the Propagation job and his way of living and his writings gave no hint as to his interest in the poor. Sheen has a scholarly, aloof intelligence and a phenomenal memory. His mind is poetic and almost mystical. However, he did not have the existential quality of a Robert Kennedy, who learned from people, rather than from books. R.F.K. had a person-to-person contact with people—he identified with the black child, the Mexican-American, the Puerto

Rican, the American Indian. Sheen always seemed aloof from the common man and not part of the mainstream of human living.

Judging from his oratorical skill, many thought that Sheen would be a leading light at the Vatican Council II. He remained silent at the first three sessions. At the fourth and final session, he gave a dramatic plea for the Third World to a hushed espiscopal audience. Many of them thought him too dramatic—preaching, in a sense, to the preachers. His thesis was: "As Chastity was the fruit of the Council of Trent, Obedience the fruit of the First Vatican Council, so let the Spirit of Poverty be the fruit of the Second Vatican Council."

"We live in a world," he said, "in which 200 million people would willingly take the vow of poverty tomorrow, if they could live as well, eat as well, be clothed as well, and be housed as well as I am, or even as some who take the vow of poverty."

Some found Sheen too histrionic; priests especially were not his greatest admirers. This must be said of him: the poor throughout the world are grateful to this extraordinary man. From 1950 to his going to Rochester in 1966, he headed an organization that sent $200 million to the needy overseas. The leper in a leper colony in Korea, the starving child in India, the stricken T.B. victim in the bush of Africa, will never know their benefactor, Fulton J. Sheen, who has succeeded in awakening the conscience of America to the problems of the Third World. He was a

Poverty Program all on his own, years before it was a popular thing to do. Was he a prophet again, ahead of his time, or was it a question of the needs of the singer and not the nature of the song?

In the sixties Latin America became of particular interest to Sheen. I remember well in 1960 when he came to Buenos Aires in Argentina for a great crusade. He was a tremendous success. He was on TV and he preached in the Cathedral. He went to Rio in Brazil and spoke there on television.

Latin America is nominally Catholic. There is no middle class there, only the haves and the have-nots. The haves have too much; the have-nots have much too little. In Rio de Janeiro they call them "favelas," in Buenos Aires "Banda de miseria," in Peru "barriadas," in Bogota "tigurios." Call them what you want, they are soul-searing slums that cluster around the great cities of Latin America. They are misery at its worst. Death is easy and often a merciful exit. Hunger and pain are facts of everyday life. The Church in Latin America has not put itself on the line in combating poverty.

Although Sheen was one of the first to bring the needs of the poor to America's attention, he however never became the champion of the Third World movement led by his friend the diminutive and aggressive Archbishop Helder Camara of Recife in Brazil, gently dubbed "The Red Archbishop" by Pope John. Recife is one of the poorest areas in the world and has one of the most difficult climates. Camara was formerly auxiliary bishop in Rio. He lived and

worked in the favelas, among the million poor perched outside the tourist mecca. Camara is different from Sheen in
that he lived among the poor and experienced poverty himself. He is world known because of his devotion to the
poor and his championship of the underdeveloped regions
of the world. For his backing of the poor he has now the
enmity of conservative interests in Church and State. At-
tempts have been made on his life. It is the eleventh hour in
Latin America. It is an awakening giant. Violence seems inevitable. That is why the slain priest, rebel son of wealthy
parents, Camilo Torres, whom many consider a martyr, and
the rebel Che Guevara are held in high esteem.

Sheen never really understood and certainly never accepted Guevara's philosophy. Che Guevara was no insane
fanatic. He did not possess a pathological love of bloodshed
and cruelty. He was an idealist who rebelled against the
established order of things. He was a man deeply moved
by the rampant social injustices he saw all around him in
Latin America. He attempted to rectify the evils he saw
about him and in doing so he became a kind of folk hero,
the revolutionary par excellence. He tried to make a heaven
right here on earth. He was a brave and courageous man
who gave his life for his ideals. A Latin American priest
commented at his death: "To pass one's life in the jungle—
ill clothed and starving—with a price on his head—confront-
ing the military power of imperialism—sick with asthma—
exposing himself to death by suffocation—if the bullets did
not cut him down first. A man who could have lived regally

with money, amusements, friends, women and vices in any
of the great cities of Sin—this is heroism—true heroism no
matter how confused or wrong his ideas might have been."

The physician Guevara is a reminder to the Church in
Latin America of its unfilled duty to the masses, its failures
to promote some kind of Christian socialism.

Camara has said, "Human alienation can result either
from ignoring time in favor of eternity, or from ignoring
eternity, in favor of time. They are the two faces of alienation." On either score, Camara is certainly not an alienated
man.

The chief revolutionary force in Brazil is not the students
or organized labor or any of the traditional leftist parties,
but the Roman Catholic Church, or rather its progressive
wing. Hundreds of Brazilian priests and bishops are struggling not only against strict Church orthodoxy, but also,
of greater and more immediate significance, against the
military-sponsored controlled government. It is they and
not any political party who lead the opposition against the
ruling regime. Sheen on the other hand was always part of
the civic and religious institution. He hardly ever challenged political and religious bureauocrats.

They have made it clear, however, that they do not
merely wish to sweep the military from power, but to see
enacted radical social and economic reforms which would
in effect destroy the existing order. The rebel movement
within the Latin American Church is epitomized by its foremost leader and exponent, Helder Camara. He has expressed

publicly his sympathy and admiration for the slain Che Guevara. Echoing Che, he says, he sees Brazil as Latin America's Vietnam and in late 1968 took what may be a beginning in the area of social revolution. He organized a movement called Acao–Justicia Y Paz Action–Justice and Peace. The purpose of AJP, as it is called, is "to prove with deeds that in no wise will stop at reformism but demand a structural transformation." Sounding very much like Che, Camara insists his movement seeks peaceful change, "but if after having exhausted all our efforts we cannot make the powers that be concede anything—then if armed revolution comes that would not be our responsibility." He adds that although his movement will try to steer clear of armed revolution, it will "respect those who in all conscience opt for armed violence."

Sheen, as well as Camara, have been shocked by what is called the tragic split in much of our religious outlook between the saved and the secular, the Church and human society. Dietrich Bonhoeffer, the martyred Lutheran theologian, brutally hanged by the Gestapo in 1945, recognized this split in his Church. For him, the German Christian's support of Hitler's Aryan madness was the supreme condemnation of the radical separation in much of Christianity between law and gospel. As Camara so aptly puts it, "All those who accept the truth of the gospel in their lives are called to plan their part in the defense of man and of justice."

Dr. Allende, a professed Marxist, through his election by

the ballot rather than by the bullet to the presidency of Chile, is an indictment of the Church's failure to lead a Christian social revolution "South of the Border." Surprisingly, Allende has openly indicated his admiration for the late Pope John XXIII and he has expressed the hope that his coalition policies will "make the gospels of Christ a reality."

When Sheen was appointed to Rochester, Cardinal Spellman expressed his deep respect and admiration for the extraordinary talents with which God had blessed the Archbishop: ". . . all those talents and every ounce of his energy he has dedicated to the missions—to spreading Christ's kingdom across the wide world and begging for God's needy everywhere. What he has done for the missions can never be measured, but it is certain in every part of the world his name is held in grateful memory by countless thousands."

Sheen was a champion of the poor abroad. What position did he and his Church take at home in the question of race minority groups and hunger? Cesar Chavez has said: "To be a man is to suffer for others. God help us to be men." Does the Church put itself on the line in these United States in the matter of human dignity? Sheen and his Church were always talking about the poor overseas; it was only in November 1970 the American bishops launched an intensive campaign for human development, entitled *"For God's Sake."* Its goal was $50 million and its aim was, to quote Pope Paul's words, *"to break the hellish cycle of poverty."* Its purpose was to help the very young and the very old who cannot help themselves. Its purpose also was to help the others to help themselves. It was given top priority by the bishops. The campaign will reach out to help the twenty-five million Americans who live below the poverty line. It is headed by Bishop Dempsey, auxiliary bishop of Chicago—a man who has devoted thirty years of his life to the Chicago ghettoes. Some think this effort is too little and too late.

In his early days in Rochester, Sheen spoke to the city's Chamber of Commerce. "I am one of your latest citizens, but one of your proudest. Look what we do: we help clothe the world; we photograph the world; we make precise the imprecisions of the rest of the world. There is not a single problem in the technological field which we cannot solve." This in a few words described the smug self-image of itself the city of Rochester had. These were the best times for some. These were the worst times for others.

But then Sheen said other things. He said that the Church had failed to meet the great religious, social, and secular crises of history, because it had failed to read the signs of the times. "As the Church had to learn that the world was the stage on which the gospel was preached, so the world had to learn that the inner city is the area where the secular city will find God. The whole world looks at Rochester but it does not see the city's beauty; it sees the blemish on its face." He did not have to elaborate on "the blemish." He clearly meant the condition of the unemployed, ill-housed, uneducated Negro poor. There are a thousand

Rochesters in our great land. Where does the Church stand?

Where was the Church in the Civil Rights Movement? Certainly nuns, priests, and laymen marched shoulder to shoulder with Dr. Martin Luther King along the dusty sunsoaked roads of Alabama. Martin Luther King was an extraordinary man, who for one brief moment, through the sheer magnificence of his personality, managed to convince, Jew, Catholic, and Protestant, black and white, that together we could overcome, we could cure the cancerous hate that is destroying the bloodstream of American life. But that moment did not last. His dream became a nightmare. Dr. King was one of the first men of prestige in the country to speak out against the Vietnamese war. He must certainly rank among the greats of these United States. Those of us who work in the inner cities know that the minority groups are crushed by frustration, oppression, despair, and apathy. Where to turn? To the institutional Church? No. To the President, who apparently has not much empathy for the young or the black poor, whose philosophy is a "malignant neglect"? There is an old hymn which says, "Once to every man and nation there comes a moment to decide." Now is that moment for our Church to give the leadership necessary. The Church has to back the Groppis, the Abernathys—all those who try to make the Church relevant in the world. Sheen has been a champion of the poor, yet in his own life he never really identified with them.

Sheen said, "Never before in the history of the world

was there a Church as rich as the Church in the United States. By rich we do not mean luxurious, as in the sense of the Renaissance, nor selfishly comfortable, nor that the bishops and priests live in a manner that scandalizes the people; but rich in the sense of living in the most prosperous civilization with which God has ever blessed the earth. May we be gutted when they are gutted. We must become the Church of the poor, or else we will become the poor Church."

Sheen joined the most exclusive club in the world—the Roman Catholic hierarchy—in May 1951, at age fifty-six, rather old for a man of his great ability. He was in Germany speaking to the American soldiers when it was announced that Pope Pius XII had appointed him titular Bishop of Caesariana and one of Spellman's twelve apostles, as auxiliary Bishop of New York. He was ordained a bishop on June 11, 1951, by Cardinal Piazza, the then secretary of the Consistorial Congregation which chooses and supervises the bishops of the world. The ordination took place in the Church of Sts. John and Paul, the Church in Rome of which Spellman was titular head. I heard Sheen say later, when he was on Spellman's black list, that the reason he was ordained bishop in Rome was that he did not want Spellman to officiate.

After the ceremony Pope Pius received the new bishop for a long private audience. It was known in Vatican circles at the time that when Pope Pius referred to Sheen, he always called him Fulton. Sheen saw the Pope yearly for a half-hour audience until the Pontiff died. It is a mystery he never gave Sheen a prestigious position in the Church. Apparently he sided with the man from Boston in the Spellman-Sheen feud. There is a price on everything in life. To achieve promotion in the Church, would Sheen be prepared to pay that price?

CHAPTER

5

THE MICROPHONE OF GOD

SHEEN, the friend of the colorful mayor of New York, James Walker, and of the Happy Warrior, Al Smith, in 1930 became the first preacher of the "Catholic Hour," a regular Sunday program at 6 P.M. He gave a series of talks entitled "The Divine Romance" which dealt with the basic doctrines of the Catholic Church. Several Catholic newspapers did not like the program. They considered it rather highbrow and suited only for the classroom. Amos and Andy were highly popular at that time. One newspaper suggested that Father Sheen be taken off the air and be replaced by something like Amos and Andy who would present the Church's position in a semihumorous vein. Sheen, however, remained a regular on the "Catholic Hour" from 1930 to 1952. Two popes recommended topics to him. Pius XI suggested he talk out against communism; Pope Pius XII recommended talks on certain aspects of the Church.

Once a check was made on the amount of letters received over a three month period while Sheen was on the "Catholic Hour." The total number was about seven hundred thousand. For more than twenty years Sheen gave the Lenten sermons each year in New York until he was on Spellman's black list. Sheen, at Cardinal Cooke's invitation, gave the Good Friday talk in St. Patrick's, New York, in 1970 and again in 1971. Spellman's heir apparent was presumably not carrying on the vendetta.

Sheen has traveled in all the states lecturing and preaching. He has journeyed the world over. Some years ago he gave more than two hundred talks when he made a forty-day tour with Cardinal Spellman, speaking in Australia, New Zealand, China, Japan, the Pacific islands, Vietnam, Korea, and Southeast Asia. Sheen never used notes for his talks except when he was required to produce a text for the "Catholic Hour." He believed that a preacher who uses notes is about as effective as a man proposing to a girl from a notebook. He tells the story of a woman who once saw a bishop reading a sermon and remarked: "Glory be to God. If he can't remember it, how does he expect us to?"

When Sheen was at the Catholic University he was chaplain to an orphanage. His custom was to rise each day at 5 A.M. and walk to the orphanage, giving sermons out loud, addressing his words to the telephone poles and trees. In this way he developed a beautiful voice which some will claim was second only to the golden baritone voice of Charles Coughlin, the radio priest from Detroit. One Good Friday in Westminster Cathedral in London, England, some twenty thousand people, most of whom overflowed into the streets, listened to Sheen preach a sermon on "The Seven Last Words."

In the 1920's and the early 1930's a household word in America was the radio priest, Father Charles Coughlin. He was pastor of the Shrine of the Little Flower in Royal Oak, Michigan. From his office atop the church tower he used to broadcast his talks. Royal Oak became a tourist attraction, Charles Coughlin a controversial character. Coughlin was a kindly man, big in stature and like Sheen a master of the air waves. The basis for Coughlin's success was a beautiful baritone voice. His diction was flawless. His rolling R's were intriguing. He was a master of alliteration and beautiful imagery. Although his style was distinct from Sheen's, the popular appeal of the one was like that of the other twenty-five years later on TV. For three years Coughlin preached the gospel, then branched into politics. He attacked the Hoover Administration and backed F.D.R. Coughlin's slogan was: "It's Roosevelt or Ruin. The New Deal is Christ's Deal." Then Coughlin tired of Roosevelt—it was a clash between two egocentrics. In 1936 Coughlin called Roosevelt "a liar," "A Communist," and "Franklin Double Cross Roosevelt." In 1936 Eugenio Cardinal Pacelli visited the United States. Francis Spellman, the then Auxiliary Bishop of Boston, was his escort. Some claim that Spellman prevailed on Pacelli to have Coughlin silenced. Spellman and Roosevelt were great friends. Many would claim that Coughlin was a finer preacher than Sheen.

Sheen made the transition from radio to television. The year was 1952. The place was Manhattan's crowded Adelphi Theater, off Broadway, in New York City. "Twenty seconds," an excited voice said. "Five seconds. One." Gentle music filled the tense air. An impressive man strutted out from the wings. He wore a black cassock with red piping, red cape flowed from his shoulders, as from those of a *torero*. On his chest was an impressive gold cross. He looked taller than he really was. He bowed to the crowd and said, "Thank you for allowing me into your home once again." A microphone like the sword of Damocles dangled above his head. The resonant tones of his voice boomed in the still air. The voice belonged to His Excellency Fulton J. Sheen, Auxiliary of New York, the most famous preacher of the twentieth century. A new TV star was born. Sheen was beginning his most successful role. He is without a doubt one of the most remarkable men ever to grace a TV screen.

Sheen was keenly conscious of the impact his TV appearance had, but he used to enjoy this joke on himself. He tells of a woman in Brooklyn who saw him marching in procession outside a Church and was unimpressed, remarking, "You don't look nearly as good as you do on TV."

The Bishop Sheen show, called "Life is Worth Living," was a half-hour program on such diverse subjects as war, Stalin, psychiatry, the psychology of the Irish, the Divine sense of humor. The talks were a kind of Christian humanism, not commercials for the Roman Catholic Church, but designed to suit people of all faiths and of none. The Dumont Network, which presented the initial program free of charge, gave Sheen an obituary spot, opposite two highly rated national shows—Mr. Television, Milton Berle, and the Man from Hoboken, Frank Sinatra. The day and time were Tuesdays at 8 P.M.

Sheen was a spectacular success. Dumont was overwhelmed with mail, about ten thousand letters a week. The first programs were then carried by seventeen stations. Berle's ratings suddenly dropped about ten points. One TV critic attributed it to Sheen. Berle quipped, "If I'm going to be eased off TV by anyone, it's better that I lose to the One for Whom Bishop Sheen is speaking." In the New York Archdiocese at that time, a standard question among the priests at supper on Tuesdays was "Who are you going to watch tonight—Uncle Miltie or Uncle Fultie?"

Some people were aghast to encounter a bishop on a TV screen. Sheen saw nothing extraordinary about it. He had been broadcasting for twenty-five years on the radio, twenty-two of them on the "Catholic Hour." He had uttered unlimited words, from testimonials to fashionable weddings. He spoke in the bush of Africa, in the slums of Latin America, and in the most beautiful cathedrals in the world. He talked at street corners in Alabama. He would have preached from the housetops at Christ's injunction if the occasion arose. So the transition from the radio to the television was a natural one for the missionary with a mike,

God's press agent, Fulton J. Sheen. Sheen's TV program was no religious "Sesame Street." Some found it too philosophical.

Sheen was way ahead of Vatican Council II as regards the ecumenical movement. He was not trying to convert America to Catholicism. His program was not a dogmatic one, but a mixture of common sense, logic, and Christian ethics. It could be called "Instant Religion." He spoke before a live audience of eleven hundred people and three TV cameras. Wearing light-tan powder over his makeup base, he talked for twenty-eight minutes to the second, without script, notes, or cue cards of any sort. He said, "Always know where you are going to end. It may be a paragraph or a sentence, but know how long it's going to take to say it. Then watch the clock. When there's just enough time for the conclusion—say it, and you've finished on time."

Loretta Young, a friend of Sheen's, called him the greatest orator of our time. His voice has a tinge of the brogue, and a mixture of Oxford and American, and can vary from a spine-tingling whisper to an Old Testament fury. His hands used to touch the chain of his cross, spread outward in supplication, saw the air, or shoot upwards to emphasize a point. He had no props, just a blackboard on which he frequently wrote. He used anecdotes and well-worn jokes. Whenever a stagehand out of camera range wiped the blackboard clean, Sheen referred to him as "my little angel." It became a running gag, and Sheen used to say of his angel,

"He pays no taxes, he has no visible means of support."
"My angel," he says, "used angel shampoo." One night
Sheen hailed a taxi in New York City. The driver recognized him. "Bishop Sheen," he said, "I love your program
on TV. It's an education. I pick up so many big words
listening to it. You have a marvelous voice; there is so much
animosity in it." Sheen's sudden rise to fame, however, did
not delight everyone, especially his priest colleagues. Some
found him too "Hollywood" for their taste. He was, nevertheless, at that time on good terms with Spellman, and
gradually being groomed for higher things, until their feud
put an end to all that. Also at that time he was held in high
esteem by the Vatican, attested to by the following comment of one of their maverick unnamed spokesmen, "He
is our right hand in the U.S.A." Even Pope Pius XII followed his telecasts faithfully. The man from Peoria had
come a long way and his future looked bright.

Sheen's "Life is Worth Living" series was probably one
of the most extraordinary productions ever to appear on
television. It was such a success on the Dumont channel it
had to move to ABC to get a national hookup. NBC and
CBS had turned it down, much to their regret later on. It
reached an estimated twenty-five million viewing audience
in 1954, quite a following at that time; it would be equiva-
lent to sixty million today. One of the tragedies of Sheen's
life and the Church he served so well is that it never used
his immense talents. He was a veritable priest-worker who
was a real professional in a most influential media, and yet

the Church never gave him the backing and the openings he so richly deserved. He was never at peace in the Church, yet like most of us, he could never leave it.

The Admiral Corporation were his earthly sponsors. Some people thought it strange to see a bishop plugging their radios, refrigerators, TV sets, and air conditioners. The program began with a commercial, continued with an uninterrupted talk, another commercial, and a brief reappearance by the Bishop when he gave his plug for the poor of the world. In 1951–1953 Sheen was paid $10,000 a telecast by Admiral. It was increased to $12,000 and $14,000 in successive seasons. In 1955 Admiral paid him $16,500 for each telecast for twenty-six shows. Sheen gave all these fees to the Propagation of the Faith for the poor overseas.

Although the talk was not really rehearsed, Sheen put about thirty hours of preparation into the half-hour appearance, coming up with enough material for five or six hours. He was fastidious about the lighting and the camera work. His eyes are magnetic; he insisted they be underlit, so they would look like dark, glowing coals. He usually began his preparation five or six days ahead, writing notes and ideas on yellow pads. He then would call some of his associates, for some ideas about jokes. He had an old joke book himself. Then he would give the talk in Italian at the Convent of the Franciscan Sisters on Forty-fifth Street in New York City. Sometimes he would give it in French to a friend. Sheen was then ready to face his hosts of fans on Tuesday evening through the medium of TV.

His show was really unpredictable. At one moment, he was humorous. Another moment he would write on the blackboard. Then he would stride toward the cameras, eyes blazing, declaiming as a twentieth-century Savanarola. He had a great sense of humor. He might suddenly recount a story that Harry Hirshfield told about the uncertainty for commuters on the Long Island Railroad. A man had a heart seizure on the train on the way home one evening. A priest was called to give him the last rites, and said to him, "My good man, you are dying, you better make your peace with God. You are going either to Heaven or to Hell." The man looked up at the priest and said, "Father, I don't care where I am going, as long as I don't have to change at Jamaica."

Another story he used over and over was of the time he was to give a lecture at a certain hotel. He arrived rather late, and there was no time to eat. Some of the organizers of the event took him to the hotel cafeteria to grab a quick snack of graham crackers and a glass of milk. A flippant young thing in her early thirties turned to the Bishop, looked at him all decked out in his red robes, and said, "What will you have, Cock Robin?" Some people found Sheen arrogant; of course, he had a lot to be arrogant about. He was a miracle on TV. Here was a man of God very much at home on Madison Avenue. He could compete with "pros" in their own medium, could equal the best, and was better than most of them. Sheen suited the various demands of his audience: cerebral with the intellectuals, flattering to the ladies, and folksy for the common man. In 1955 his TV program was carried by 170 stations in the United States, and 17 in Canada. The viewers were in this order—Jewish, Protestant, and Catholic.

Sheen, unlike Marshall McLuhan, did not believe the medium was the message. Sheen's thesis has been: If you want people to stay as they are, you tell them what they want to hear. If you want to improve them, you tell them what they should know. Like the splendid communicator Edward R. Murrow, Sheen regarded TV as a sound-equipped mirror, reflecting the good and bad in society.

What brought Sheen to TV? The realization that by that means he could reach more people in half an hour than St. Paul reached in all his missionary journeys. In 1957, when under pressure from Spellman Sheen retired from the TV screens, his audience included a great many of the seventy million Americans whom surveys indicate never go to church.

Sheen—off TV for two years—came back again in 1959. He quipped, "Long time, no Sheen." Asked to explain his phenomenal success on TV, he said, "The Lord once used an ass to ride into Jerusalem. Now he uses an ass on TV." Sheen once received an Emmy Award on the same evening one was given to Bob Hope. On receiving his trophy, Hope quipped, "I want to thank my writers." Sheen stepped up to the microphone and said, "I want to thank my writers too—Matthew, Mark, Luke, and John."

As an inspirational spellbinder in the twentieth century

there hasn't been anybody around like Sheen. His program was Instant College. In the preparation of his telecast, Sheen was aware that the Catholic, the Protestant, the Jew, the Communist, the Agnostic, and the Skeptic all would be listening to him. That is why he used a common denominator and worked up the ladder to the Divine—until, at the end, he would reach a spiritual truth.

Sheen proved that a great teacher is as fascinating a personality as a Berle, a Crosby, or a Chevalier, a Streisand, or a Sinatra. Whereas they needed an orchestra, some props, and a bevy of writers, Sheen required only listeners. His music came in the form of a powerful, resonant, voice machine. His props were a pair of deep-socketed, hypnotic eyes and expressive hands; Most of his writers, Matthew, Thomas of Aquin, Socrates, were long since dead. With these Sheen put together a performance in which he emerged as an inspirational spellbinder, yet his Church never used to the full his extraordinary gifts.

The best known of Sheen's books, *Peace of Soul*, provided him with a favorite anecdote. "Did you hear," he said, eyes twinkling, "about the nice woman who went into Brentano's bookstore and asked for Rabbi Sheen's *A Piece of My Mind?*" Sheen has been a prolific writer. He has written about seventy books, a few of which were best sellers. His writings have been much influenced by the style of G. K. Chesterton, and the influence of Bernard Shaw is also evident, particularly in his use of paradox. At times, Sheen seems to sacrifice and stretch the truth for dramatic effect. He writes as he talks, in the rather flowery style of a preacher.

Since Vatican Council II his impact as a writer has considerably diminished. The forthright presentation of a Eugene Kennedy, a Hans Kung, a Karl Rahner, and an Yves Congar has certainly tolled the death knell for the poetic approach of Sheen. These men define the gut issues and the challenges of the last third of the twentieth century in cold prose.

Sheen once gave a retreat for the monks in the Abbey of Gethsemane in Kentucky. The most famous member of that community was the late Thomas Merton—known in religious life as Fr. Louis—who met his untimely death in the Far East by a faulty electric wire. He was taken from us at the time we could little afford his loss. He was one of the most famed writers in America. His autobiography, *The Seven Story Mountain,* published in 1948, gave an account of his life before he entered the monastery, and is not only a best-selling work which many found inspiring, it is also a singularly glowing piece of English prose. Sheen said of *The Seven Story Mountain,* "The autobiography of Thomas Merton is a twentieth-century form of the *Confessions of St. Augustine.*" Merton matured and grew as a writer. At his death he was becoming really socially involved. He was against the war in Vietnam; he was a champion of civil rights and the poor; he was for optional celebacy;—but he never had the impact or influence of Sheen.

Thomas Merton was one of the revolutionary thinkers of our age. His whole life was a constant search: he dug deeper and deeper into the human mind and soul. When he joined the Trappists in the early 1940's his spirituality was based on a severe and negative, rather harsh, seventeenth-century approach to religion. There was a tremendous growth in his work. His crusade for world peace and his deep interest in oriental spirituality gave witness to that. His research in the latter led him to his rendezvous with the wire that electrocuted him in Bangkok. After *The Seven Story Mountain*, an intense spiritual Odyssey, he returned in his writings to the basic issues of our time: poverty, war and peace, nonviolence, and racial justice. Black Panther leader Eldridge Cleaver read *The Seven Story Mountain* while he was in prison. Merton saw nonviolence as the only answer in the quest for a lasting peace in a confused world perpetually at war. Shortly before his death he published an essay on nonviolence which, incidentally, he had dedicated to the pacifist folk singer Joan Baez, who had just visited him at Gethsemane Monastery. In this essay he lists four conditions for an honest nonviolence. One: It must be "aimed, above all at the transformation of the present state of the world." Two: For him practicing it, it must be "clearly not for himself, but for others—that is, for the poor and underprivileged." Three: "Above all—nonviolence must avoid a facile and fanatical self-righteousness." Four: It must be free from the need to see "immediate—visible results." Merton was never limited solely to religious topics. His constant anguish was the paradox of the human condition with its agonies and ecstacies. His pilgrimage was that continuous search for peace of soul which each one must possess; otherwise one dies years before one is buried. It was that pilgrimage that brought him to Bangkok and that electric wire that blackened his skin and stopped his noble heart. Fulton Sheen was the Merton of the religious mass media, but did his awful need for adulation and personal acceptance deprive him of the solitude and inner tranquillity so necessary to be great?

There is no noticeable growth in Sheen's writings. An honest, frank autobiography of Sheen could be one of the most powerful documents in all Church history. The crisis in the Church today is not one of faith; it's one of honesty. Men like Sheen should speak up, and people yet unborn will be spared the agonies many of us go through because of the present structures in the Church. Freedom and honesty are vital. As a Danish poet put it, "The noble art of losing face will one day save the human race"—and the churches too.

One of Sheen's best books is his *Life of Christ*. It is an account of the greatest life ever lived, and the most moving story ever told. It is a magnificent portrayal of Christ as a man, as a teacher, as the Saviour. The familiar incidents and figures of the New Testament are brought dramatically to life. New light is thrown on old passages. It is not a scholarly, but a popular work. Sheen said of this book, "It is hoped that the author's sweet intimacy with the crucified Christ which time brought will break through these pages, giving to the reader the peace which God alone can bring." This book was written when the feud between Spellman and Sheen had almost reached an impasse.

A passage from the same work which points out the influence of Chesterton is the following. The scene is Calvary. Christ is dying. A thief being crucified with him asks for forgiveness. Sheen continues, "A dying man asked a dying man for eternal life. A man without possessions asked a poor man for a kingdom. A thief at the door of death asked to die like a thief and steal paradise. One would have thought a saint would have been the first soul purchased over the counter of Calvary by the red coins of Redemption. But in the Divine Plan, it was a thief who was the escort of the King of Kings into Paradise."

Sheen is a popular writer. For a long time it has been fashionable to have some of Sheen's books in a conspicuous place in one's library. He has not really made a great contribution to literature, but he has a pleasing, catchy style.

It is difficult for Sheen these days. A man who had his own radio and TV shows, a man who has written seventy books, must now be satisfied to do the rounds of the talk shows, to visit with the Merv Griffins, David Frosts, Mike Douglases, Dick Cavetts, and Johnny Carsons in order to reach the public. Now we need a man of the caliber of Sheen to be a translator and an interpreter of what is going on—but he has no platform.

CHAPTER

6

THE PRICE

THE FIERY young Irish rebel, Bernadette Devlin, wrote in her autobiography, *"The Price of My Soul* refers not to the price for which I would be prepared to sell out, but rather to the price we all must pay in life to preserve our own integrity. To gain that which is worth having, it may be necessary to lose everything else."

It was October 28, 1969, 10 P.M. EST in the CBS television studio, New York. "Sixty Minutes," a TV program, had just begun. The host of the show was Mike Wallace. Under the bright, hot lights of the cameras, he was then questioning a man whose face was known to millions of viewers. After an absence of nine years from screens in homes around the country, Archbishop Fulton J. Sheen had returned.

He had just resigned as Bishop of Rochester. Under Wallace's adroit questioning, Sheen revealed some of the disturbing facets of his life and times. If the Roman Catholic Church is viewed as a macrocosm, then Fulton Sheen is a microcosm that reveals the soul of the Church.

His interview that night provided more questions than answers. Why Sheen had failed to receive a cardinal's hat was Wallace's first question. Sheen replied, "It is possible for a man in the Church to go up and up, and I would have gone higher and higher and higher."

Mike Wallace: "But . . ."

Sheen: "But I refused to pay the price."

Wallace: "And that would be?"

Sheen: "Well, I felt it would be disloyalty to my own principles, and I think to Christian practice."

It is a pity that Sheen did not speak up on nationwide TV, but the price to which he referred, as those of us who worked with him so well knew, was submission to the will of the late Cardinal Spellman of New York.

As many before me who prayed and obeyed, I once considered the Roman Church the most unshakable rock in a turbulent world. Today, as do others, I find many cracks in its foundation. For me, as for others growing up within its cloak of security, the Church offered changeless sameness; for the weak and thoughtless, comforting rules, unquestionable obedience, a faith that consoled rather than challenged. It was a kind of spiritual fire insurance. It spoke about the pie in the sky. Put up with things here—things will be better in the hereafter. Fear, rather than love, was the condition for membership.

I found, too, that the laymen of the Church were

basically good, simple, hardworking people. The absolute loyalty to, and respect for, their clergy prohibited them from even entertaining the thought of questioning the activities or pronouncements of a pastor, let alone a bishop, or, heaven forbid, the Pope, who walked in the shoes of Peter, while they had to walk in their own.

I have often seen, during the quiet hours of the day, pious Catholic women slip away from their home duties to make a visit to the Church. They would sit in the semi-darkness of God's house under a flickering votive light and finger their beads. Afterward, they might spend an hour or two mending altar linens or waxing the altar floor. It was considered an honor to work for God, and they did it with eagerness.

Once a month the men of the parish Holy Name Society would attend mass in a body and then march from the church to the school cafeteria for breakfast and an innocuous speech by a local sportsman, fireman, or policeman.

Catholics raised their children to be clean and obedient like themselves, always sent them to parochial schools, and felt their highest honor as parents was having one of their children choose a vocation as a priest or as a nun. Their next aim was to bring as many persons as possible into the Church, thereby insuring for themselves a place in Heaven.

Beyond their parish community lay the chancery office, and beyond that—Rome. And the chancery was responsible only to Rome, and the Pope only to God.

In this light, it is easier for us to comprehend how this

emotional climate permitted the shepherd to have unlmited control over the sheep—control which ultimately fostered infighting, behind closed doors, in a power struggle among the shepherds. The thirst for power among the priests, monsignors, bishops, and cardinals went totally unchecked, simply because there was no one to check it. Michael Novak has said, "Ambition is the ecclesiastical lust."

Quarrels and vendettas could, and did, undermine the basic structure of the Church, and its direction. Ultimately, it was the people who suffered. As I endeavor to tell the events that occurred among some of the Church's hierarchy, it is not to criticize the men, but to take a hard look at them as victims—victims of the psychology that nurtured and shaped them. They were men incapable, because of their lack of real freedom and intellectual honesty, of reacting in any way but the way they did.

The psychology that shaped them is the very psychology poked and probed at by the "Fat Christ," Pope John, in his effort to renew the personality of the Church, by analyzing the life style that had permitted the interior battle to occur at the cost of men.

Two giants in the American Catholic Church were the late Francis Cardinal Spellman of New York, and Archbishop Fulton J. Sheen. As I see it, the problems within each of these men, and the problems between them, epitomize some of the causes of the problems within the Church. The feud that erupted between these two shepherds was to become one of the most revealing in all Church history.

Cardinal Spellman, who influenced Church affairs in the United States for more than twenty-five years, was a short, rotund man, with a cherubic face that masked an iron will. He was a great friend; he was a terrible enemy. Widely known at home, and a constant visitor to the far corners of the world, he was a kind of Yankee pope. Spellman's seat of power was located in an opulent Victorian structure on Madison Avenue in New York, the New York Archdiocesan chancery office. Analagous to the home office of a major corporation, it was from this base of operations that Spellman cultivated enduring friendships with the politically powerful figures of his time. Counted among his close friends were presidents of the United States, from Roosevelt to Johnson, senators, congressmen, mayors, corporate leaders, and the wealthy. Spellman was a powerful man. During his time he was rated second only to the Pope.

For many years in the Vatican there was a fastidious tendency to identify Catholicism with Europe. The well-known English writer Hilaire Belloc once observed, "Europe is the faith, and the faith is Europe." As late as 1908 the United States was deemed by Rome a missionary territory. Many of its priests were imports, and foreign monies were necessary to support its activities.

For a century, United States bishops were chosen by Rome's Society for the Propagation of the Faith. Those selected were almost always French or Irish. Catholicism in the United States labored under a widespread suspicion of being an alien creed. Some believed that the Church would only prosper by doing its utmost to Americanize the immigrants, and adapt its policy to that of the young democracy. A problem still in the American Church today is that it has still many of the Old World Puritan ideals, and is ruled strictly in the Old World fashion.

Vatican officials and other principals were not satisfied with the United States separation of Church and State: Pope Leo XIII condemned it. United States Catholics, recognized in the country as a minority, were convinced that such a separation was their life's savior. The American hierarchy disregarded them. The late great Jesuit theologian, John Courtney Murray, was under a Vatican cloud for his views on this subject, but the Document on Religious Liberty of Vatican Council II vindicated him. The happy warrior, Al Smith, once remarked, "Equality of all churches, all sects, all beliefs before the law, as a matter of right, and not as a matter of favor, I believe is the absolute separation of Church and State."

In the early twenties, Communist Russia made no amends about its implacable hostility to religion, and scarcely bothered to conceal its low regard for human life. In the thirties, Nazi Germany and Facist Italy were no better. They did not keep their concordats with Rome. All Europe was threatened by communism. To meet this crisis, the Vatican looked for ideological and material support of its policies.

To enlist United States support, it turned to the devout, uniquely American in career and character, Francis Spell-

man. Really to understand Sheen and his place in history,
it is necessary to understand Spellman and his place in
power and Church politics. Sheen was being groomed for
higher things when his friendship with the man from
Boston was shattered, and thus began his slow but sure decline on the clerical totem pole.

Spellman had influence with the people in power; Sheen
had people-power. Spellman, not an imposing figure, was
a poor speaker and an even poorer writer. However, he
had a genius all his own. He was a consummate politician.
He knew how to manipulate and use people to get what he
wanted. Sheen never had any close friends among the powers
that be and when the infighting between him and Spellman
became rough, he had no friend in court to fight his case.
He was surrounded by a few men who were opportunists,
and many women who were just camp followers, fawners
who never told him the truth about himself. They fed his
voracious appetite for adulation and attention.

Spellman was educated in public schools in Whitman,
Massachusetts. As a boy he delivered groceries, pedaled
papers, and played baseball, although in the latter he certainly was no Mickey Mantle. He was a trolley car con-
ductor at an age when most of the solemn little Italian boys
who later on would be his peers dressed in cassocks, far
removed from the bad, bad world, had already begun their
studies for the priesthood. Spellman went to Fordham University, where he was a good student. He excelled in Latin
and tried his hand at verse. He was a dandy dresser, and

liked good company. Spellman's vocation to the priesthood surprised his friends.

Boston Brahmin Cardinal O'Connell sent him to Rome to study at the North American College. He was a fair scholar and impressed an elegant professor of theology named Borgongini Duca. Spellman, even at this early age, knew how advancement comes in the Church—to be friends with somebody who knows somebody in the Vatican.

When in 1916 Spellman returned to the United States, he translated two of his mentor's Italian devotion books into English. Spellman, with his intuition, was making the first steps to notice and promotion in Rome. However, he spent the next nine years inconspicuously in the Boston chancery. O'Connell tolerated no opposition.

Back in Rome again in 1925, the first United States priest to serve as assistant to the papal secretary of state, Spellman was the chief money-getter in the project to finance a million-dollar playground erected in Rome by the Knights of Columbus. He startled the dignified Italian prelates by his prowess in boxing and team tennis. He became friends with the Brady family, a well-known, rich, and influential American family in Rome. He helped in Americanizing the Vatican press. When Mussolini came to power, the Pope was almost a prisoner of the Vatican. Fascist guards were at the Vatican gates, and Mussolini controlled the press.

Pius XI, through his Secretary of State Eugenio (Pacelli), published an encyclical attacking fascism in the following way. Pacelli called into his office the young, energetic Spellman, who was then attached to the secretariat. He handed the encyclical to him, and said, "You are to smuggle this to Paris and give it to the world press. Don't lose a moment, and don't get caught." Spellman acted in the best tradition of cloak-and-dagger diplomacy. He piled into a small, unmarked automobile and was driven directly to the airport. There he stepped aboard the first plane to Paris. The moment of touchdown Spellman handed the encyclical to the reporters. The first Mussolini heard about it was when it was telegraphed back to the Roman papers. This act of bravery deepened the friendship of the man from Boston and the patrician Roman Pacelli.

Back again in the United States in 1932, this time as auxiliary bishop to the gruff Cardinal O'Connell in Boston, Spellman pulled a bankrupt parish, Sacred Heart in Newton Center, a Boston suburb, out of the red almost overnight. More an administrator than a scholar, in 1939 he came to New York as its archbishop. New York, after Rome, was the most prestigious diocese in the world, and certainly it was the richest. Pius XI was dead. Eugenio Pacelli, as Pius XII, was filling the shoes of Peter. Cardinal Hayes, the Archbishop of New York, died in 1938. It has been said that the papers designating his successor were on the desk of Pope Pius XI to be signed. Apparently listed for New York was the well-known Dominican Archbishop McNicholas of Cincinnati who, as fate would have it, would languish in Midwestern obscurity. Pius XI died before he could sign the papers. Pius XII became Pope. He appointed his long-time friend Francis Spellman to New York's important diocese. As we've said earlier, the way to advancement in the Church is to be friends with somebody who knows, or yourself know somebody in the Vatican. Spellman went to the top. He was friends with a Pope. Cardinal O'Connell said at Spellman's appointment, "That's what happens to a bookkeeper when you teach him how to read."

During World War II, Spellman traveled widely, covering about 120,000 miles visiting the troops. He did a great deal of secret work for President Roosevelt. He even said mass in the White House. Spellman, during Pope Pius' reign, was Catholicism's Number Two man. He was a kingmaker in the United States as far as the appointing of bishops was concerned. When Spellman flew to Rome in 1946 to receive the Red Hat, he was welcomed by Pope Pius's princely nephews at the airport. His friend, and probably Pope Pius's closest lay confidante, Count Enrico Galeazzi, Governor of the Vatican staff, usually met His Eminence whenever he arrived at Fiumicino Airport in Rome.

The Church frequently in the past looked to the United States for food to relieve the hunger and despair that drive many to communism. It looked to the United States as an example of the form of government that promised the most for the survival of the Church. It looked in the past to the Americans as an idealistic people who had at last risen to their place in world affairs, and it looked to Francis Spellman, the epitome of the American Dream.

Spellman's contribution to the Church has been enormous. His era has passed since the comings and goings of the two Johns. When John Kennedy entered the White House, Catholicism in America had come of age. When Pope John XXIII entered the Vatican, Spellmanitis had run its course. Vatican II calls for a new type of bishop. The descendant of Irish grandparents, Spellman, along with many of the American Church hierarchy and clergy, reflected the mentality of his times. The Church of his youth was struggling to gain a foothold of strength and respectability in a basically suspecting and hostile environment, where one's faith had to be carefully sheltered, lest it be blown away on the winds of an alien philosophy.

A ghetto mentality prevailed, and defensiveness, a partisan loyalty, and unquestioning obedience were deemed virtues of the highest order. Spellman's aides in the chancery office were, like himself, largely first- or second-generation Irish. Facetiously referred to as the Murphia, later, during the Kennedy Administration, to be adapted to the phrase "Irish Mafia," Spellman's aides were loyal and dependable. Their parents were the hardworking people who had deluged Heaven with prayers for a priest-son. Handpicked from the Archdiocese, these aides served a carefully controlled apprenticeship, and later many were placed in prestigious spots in New York City, or strategically dotted around the country. Sometimes compared in ability to his friend and contemporary, Joseph B. Kennedy, Spellman possessed a financial acumen and superb organizational responsibility. As the diocese grew and prospered through the diligent and persistent application of these qualities, Spellman's status and influence in Rome grew accordingly. Bricks and mortar, not people, were the order of the day. This situation was not altered until many years later when Pope John set loose the forces of social change within the Church.

Fulton Sheen entered this vortex of power in the early 1950's. When Spellman plucked him from the relative obscurity of the faculty of Catholic University in Washington, handsome, articulate, intellectual, and of course Irish, Sheen required little grooming for the task envisioned for him by Spellman. There is no evidence of discord between the two men in those early days on Madison Avenue. Sheen was appointed director of the Society for the Propagation of the Faith.

The importance of this position in the Church of America cannot be overemphasized. Only recently removed from mission status, the American Church was now entering the world scene as the breadbasket of Catholicism. Contributions from American Catholics poured in under the magnetic pull of Sheen's directorship. Although a few voices were being raised inside and outside the Church about the need for a new spiritual goal, a successful organizer and fund-raiser was much more likely to rise to prominence than those who labored in the vineyard of the person-to-person ministry.

Fulton Sheen's performance as a fund-raiser was flawless,

and within a year he was elevated to the rank of bishop and became an auxiliary or assistant to Spellman. People who spoke with Sheen in those days, immediately following his appointment, could, with a little imagination, see a cardinal's hat hovering over his head. With the advent of Sheen's television series, "Life is Worth Living," all doubt about his future vanished.

During the early 50's the name of Fulton J. Sheen, as we have seen, became known in virtually every household in America. For many average Catholics he was the first visual association with a member of their Church's hierarchy. In accord with his superiors, and as an eloquent spokesman for their views, there was little question that life was worth living for Fulton Sheen in those days. For a man shut off from the human joys of sexuality, from the close ties of wife and children, his need for power, fame, and prominence took on a frightening urgency. He needed the cheering of the crowd.

Suddenly in 1957 the complexion changed. Rumors of strife between Sheen and Spellman, rumors that Sheen's increasing popularity was beginning to threaten the personality underpinnings of his sponsor and mentor became rampant. A cataclysm of events confirmed the rumors of division between the two men. First and most dramatic was Sheen's discontinuance of his national TV series. "One must occasionally retire from the lights of TV to the shadow of the cross where one is refreshed and strengthened."

Behind the appointment by Pope Pius XII in 1958 of Cardinal Stritch of Chicago to head the Propagation of the Faith in Rome, there is a human story of personality. It reflected not only the great power of the American Church, whose annual contribution to the funds of the Propagation was almost twice that of the rest of the world combined, but it also underscored the feud which erupted between the late Cardinal Spellman of New York and Fulton Sheen, the American head of the Propagation of the Faith.

The fact that for years Spellman was the Vatican's right-hand man in the United States was due not only to the importance of New York, but also to the friendships he made as a young priest in Rome with men who were later to rise very high in the Church. One of his closest friends was Count Enrico Galeazzi, who was nearer to Pope Pius XII than any other layman. He was the Vatican's chief architect and engineer, and was the contractor for the American seminary at Rome, built mainly by funds supplied by Cardinal Spellman.

To underscore Spellman's power in Rome, the story used to be told among the New York clergy that Spellman sent his aide out to purchase a tomb. On his return the aide told him that the cheapest one he could get was one for ten thousand dollars. Spellman remarked, "That's too expensive; after all, I'll be needing it for only three days."

Spellman's position seemed unassailable. The Vatican authorities had acquired the habit of consulting him, rather than any other bishop, when there was an American question to be decided. The other American bishops took their cue from Spellman, and in practice he became the Big Daddy and the Santa Claus of the American Church. Then a brilliant star called Sheen began to shine brightly in the heavens.

In his new job as director of the Society for the Propagation of the Faith in America, Sheen showed all the vim and vigor of an effective Madison Avenue organizer. Contributions to the fund soared. Under Sheen's aegis, Americans began to contribute almost two-thirds of the entire world collection. Jealousy is not unknown, even among high churchmen. And so began the feud between the commander-in-chief and his more brilliant assistant. Referring to that feud, Sheen has remarked, "Jealousy is the tribute mediocrity pays to genius." Someone humorously commented, "They began to hate each other—for the love of God." Sheen was suddenly dropped from national TV. The priests of the New York Archdiocese were told that they would incur Cardinal Spellman's displeasure were they to invite the "Microphone of God" to preach before their congregations. Suddenly Sheen's annual invitation to preach to an overpacked St. Patrick's Good Friday service was dropped too. To deliver the Lenten sermons, he went to Jersey City, across the river, out of Spellman's jurisdiction.

Details of the feud which erupted between these two powerful men are known only to a few insiders. The act which initiated the feud is merely incidental. "Any act of disagreement or disobedience by Sheen could have been the catalyst," said one Church spokesman recently, "because sooner or later something had to cause an open conflict in what had become a cold war between them."

Spellman's most vulnerable spot turned out to be his emphasis on contributions to his well-known "Milk Fund," which was largely supported by surplus goods from the United States Government. Spellman's donation of millions of dollars' worth of surplus goods for distribution to the world's starving he gave to Sheen, and demanded millions of dollars of payment in return. Sheen refused and Spellman raged. It took some time for a full report on the situation to reach the ears of Pius XII. And then Pius acted. Both men were called to Rome. Spellman approached the Holy City with confidence. He was, after all, going to visit his friend and mentor, the man who made him what he was, and his closest personal friend. Spellman was probably the only cardinal in the world who had a direct line to the Vatican. This was used frequently for discussions of all types, including the conveyance of the Dow Jones averages, as well as the baseball scores.

Sheen was not so confident about the impending confrontation. He was a member of the most exclusive club in the world, the Bishops'. He paid his dues; he never kept the rules, however, and so, in times of crisis he was kept out of the locker room. It was beneath his dignity to play power politics.

Each man told his side of the story. Spellman, adamant

that he had paid the United States Government for the food, and Sheen equally sure that Spellman had not, and that therefore he, Sheen, was under no compulsion to pay Spellman. An inquiry was referred to Washington, and the answer came back that Spellman had indeed received the surplus food gratis.

Spellman was caught. Someone quipped jocosely about him that he would never tell a lie except for the good of the Church. Once in the web, Spellman realized he had lost face with Pope Pius XII. I remember Sheen's telling me about this incident, and Spellman's reaction. In a fit of rage he said to Sheen, "I will get even with you. It may take six months or ten years, but everyone will know what you're like."

Spellman, after that, tried to bust Sheen many times. He took his vendetta to Dunwoodie Seminary in New York where he sternly cautioned the young men studying for the priesthood that Sheen was the most disobedient priest in the country. "I want none of you to turn out like him." Spellman was instrumental in having three clerical investigations about Sheen, trying to banish him from the New York scene, and he failed.

Our Saviour's Church, on the corner of East Thirty-eighth Street and Park Avenue, New York, is a multimillion-dollar edifice. Spellman, being the shrewd businessman that he was, knew that Sheen was a successful fund-raiser and would be very helpful in paying off the great debt of that luxurious church. Sheen was appointed by Spellman its

first pastor, but he refused to accept. And so the battle
raged on. The brilliant TV personality, scholar, and orator
virtually dropped from the public view. No longer a member of the status club, he was consigned to the clerical
Siberia.

Was Sheen the victim of a clerical hatchet job, or was he
a self-destructor? Was he a masochist who had always to
be punished? He is a tortured man, and to millions of
Americans he was, at one time, a hope, but unfortunately
he lacked the courage to stand up to Spellman—that courage
which is the necessary ingredient for true greatness. Spellman, the man from Boston's Irish ghetto, had tried to bust
the man from Peoria, Illinois. The little lady saying the
Stations of the Cross in the church in Peoria, and the ex-
emplary father of ten who annually marched in the St.
Patrick's Day Parade in Boston, were oblivious to these
petty actions of the clergy, whom they held on high
pedestals. The great Australian novelist Morris L. West, in
his powerful play *The Heretic*, says: "You are horrible
men; you have no pity; you play a power game with human
lives; you crucify the Christ you say you love, in us, His
helpless children."

During the nine years of Sheen's Siberia, Pope Pius died
and was succeeded by Pope John, probably the greatest
pope in history, who reigned for a mere but vital five years
until the melancholic, Hamlet-like Pope Paul came to
power.

As abruptly as Sheen dropped out of sight, he came back

onto the scene full force when, in October 1966, Pope Paul named him Bishop of Rochester in upstate New York. Rochester, a clubby, reasonably affluent company town, would be a choice spot for a monsignor aspiring to be a bishop. Many thought the assignment of Sheen to Rochester was an insult to a man of his stature, one whose prospects, particularly earlier, prior to the feud between Spellman and Sheen, made him popularly regarded in Church circles as successor to Spellman as Archbishop of New York.

During the storm, however, Spellman's sights turned to other priests as possible successors. A man by the name of Terence Cooke rose to prominence—a company man, replacing the charismatic Sheen as a favorite son. Cooke became Spellman's devoted and closest aide. In a humorous vein, a wag quipped about their relationship, saying, "If you can't see the Captain, see the Cooke." And death, which comes to all men, came even to Spellman, and Cooke did replace him, and the clergy called it the first example of a soul-transplant.

The New York Times had a hands-off policy on Spellman. However, at his death, before he was even buried, it published a blistering editorial. It pointed out that he (Spellman) backed the late Senator Joseph McCarthy in his demagogic excesses, and made a dismaying attack on Mrs. Franklin D. Roosevelt when she upheld the separation of Church and State in education. In political affairs and in public debate he had often tended to speak in a commanding tone and to don a mask of authoritarianism which, however appropriate in some other time and some other place, was ill suited to a pluralist democracy, whether he was trying to ban the motion picture "Baby Doll" or block the reform of New York's divorce law. The editorial concluded that Cardinal Spellman sometimes squandered his own and his Church's prestige on trivial issues and lost causes.

As I have said earlier, really to know Sheen it is necessary in some sense to know Spellman. Sheen is an intolerant, spoiled, emotional, moody, cold, ambitious, and moralistic man. At times like a god of the Old Testament, but never ruthless, he is a haunted man, and basically a good man, although lacking the true ingredient to be great. Sheen did not sell out to Spellman. To preserve his integrity did he lose everything else?

Catholic power in New York City almost faded in the 1960's. It used to be an Irish city, which was synonymous with Catholic. It had power with Caesar as well as with God. It reached its apex as well as its decline under the long reign of Spellman. Spellman was more revered than loved. He was not very popular, but he was very powerful. He personally chose his successor, Terence Cardinal Cooke. It has been said that Spellman would refuse Rome to die unless this appointment came about. Cooke, however, has not the same power as Spellman; it was twilight for Irish political power in the city. Nevertheless, the influence of the Irish Mafia in ecclesiastical circles still pervades. The Italians never apparently achieved ecclesiastical eminence in New York City. The neglect of the massive influx of Spanish-speaking people in New York deprived the Catholic Church of a strong new religious and political coalition. Sheen for years was preaching the need of the have-nots overseas, neglecting to focus attention on the needs of the Puerto Ricans and the blacks in his own backyard in New York.

CHAPTER

7

PEACE OF MIND AND
PEACE OF SOUL

As IN everything else, Sheen has been ambiguous, contradictory, and unclear about his approach to psychiatry and
how to achieve peace of mind.

Sheen once said:

Anyone who had dealt closely with men will realize that, in
addition to spiritual, and moral, and intellectual problems, there
is also this overtone of the psychotic and neurotic. Now you
ask—what can be done? I am very much in favor, and I certainly practice it, of having a rigid psychiatric examination at
various periods of seminary training. Next year, for example,
according to the plans that have developed in the diocese
[Rochester] no one will be ordained, regardless of how good
they are; when they have finished their four years of training,
they are to go out in parishes for a year as deacons. Then,
after a year, they have to write in to us individually and ask
to be ordained. So, we're going to put them out in the world
and give them a test. We give them a rigid test when they enter.

I believe the Church has been recreant in the psychiatric examination of its candidates.

This interview with a veteran CBS reporter took place in October of 1969. It seems to be a reversal of Sheen's earlier approach to psychiatry. All his life he was doing battle with the psychiatrists. Some years ago, his eloquence ran away with his information on psychoanalysis, and he caused a turmoil. The psychiatrists spoke out in defense of their position. Since then, he modified his views somewhat. Two books—*Peace of Soul* and *Lift Up Your Heart* —seem to spell out his view on psychiatry. Even to this very day, however, contrary to the opinion of experts, he refuses to recognize alcoholism as a disease. In a rather risky statement, he said in a telecast some years ago, "That trend will be forgotten in thirty years."

The battle with the psychiatrists began as a result of a sermon delivered by the then Monsignor Sheen in St. Patrick's Cathedral on March 9, 1947. *The New York Times* the next morning reported that Sheen had called psychoanalysis "a form of escapism" which resulted in "morbidity and disintegration" and failed to alleviate "the unresolved sense of guilt of sin" from which most patients suffered. He charged that Freudianism was based on "materialism, hedonism, infantilism, and eroticism." Sheen's next statement was very harsh. Speaking of the transference between analyst and the client he remarked: "This method is only used when the patient is a young and very beautiful woman. It is never found to work among the ugly and the poor."

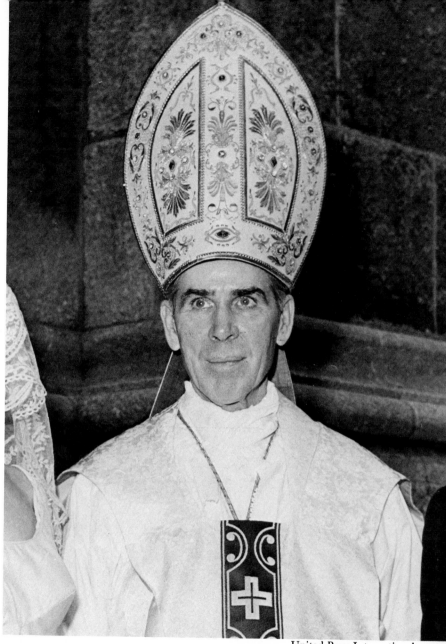

United Press International

Archbishop Fulton J. Sheen.

Religious News Service

Monsignor Sheen of the Catholic University of America, Washington, D.C. in Melbourne, Australia, where he accompanied Francis Cardinal Spellman, Archbishop of New York, for the centenary celebrations of the Melbourne Archdiocese. BELOW: *The Most Reverend Fulton J. Sheen, national director of the Society for the Propagation of the Faith, with Pope Pius XII, following Sheen's consecration as Titular Bishop of Caesariana and Auxiliary Bishop of New York in 1951.*

Religious News Service

N.C.W.C. News Service

Sheen always took a great interest in the production techniques of his famous television show "Life Is Worth Living." BELOW: *"On Camera" with "Life Is Worth Living."*

N.C.W.C. News Service

Sheen with a statue of the madonna he conceived, "Our Lady of Television."

Religious News Service

The HOLY FATHER'S

WORLDMISSION AID SOCIE

for the

PROPAGATION OF THE FAI

Bishop Sheen crusades for the Society for the Propagation of the Faith of which he was national director for many years.

Religious News Service

Cardinal Spellman presents to Sheen the gold medal of the Order of St. Sebastian, for "outstanding service to Church and country," in 1952.

United Press Photo

Sheen receives a Freedoms Foundation Award for his television program "Life Is Worth Living" in 1953. To his left is then Vice-President Richard Nixon presenting the award to Cecil B. DeMille. BELOW: *The 1952 "Man of the Year" award is presented to Sheen for his television program "Life Is Worth Living" following a poll of the country's TV editors by* Radio-Television Daily.

Religious News Service

Religious News Service

Auxiliary Bishop Sheen of New York officiates at the wedding of Archduke Rudolph of Austria and Hungary to Miss Xenia Czernichev-Besobrasov in Tuxedo Park, New York, 1953.

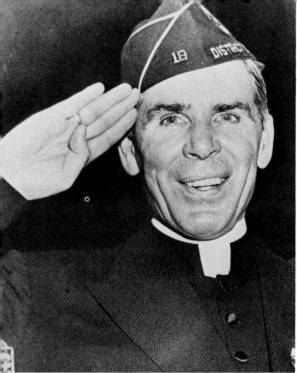

Bishop Sheen wears a Legionnaire's cap as he salutes the 39th national convention of the American Legion in 1957 at Atlantic City, N.J.

Religious News Service

A photographic portrait of Bishop Sheen.

Princess Marie Christine, seven-year-old daughter of former King Leopold and Princess Liliane of Belgium receives her first Holy Communion from Auxiliary Bishop Sheen of New York in the private chapel of the Laeken Royal Palace near Brussels in 1958.

Religious News Service

Religious News Service

Pope Pius XII chats with Auxiliary Bishop Sheen of New York during a general audience granted to national directors of the Society for the Propagation of the Faith in Vatican City, 1958.

Religious News Service

Pope John XXIII poses with Sheen following a private audience in the Vatican in 1962.

United Press International Photo

N.C.W.C. News Service

Bishop Sheen (left) and Alabama Governor George Wallace with Representative Emanuel Celler, Chairman of the House Judiciary Committee (center) before whom, in 1964, they attacked the Supreme Court decision forbidding prayers in public schools.

Cardinal Spellman and Bishop Sheen in the later days of their stormy relationship.

Religious News Service

Bishop Sheen of Rochester confers with Pope Paul VI at a private audience which preceded the opening of the Synod of Bishops in Vatican City, 1967.

Sheen with Pope Paul VI who appointed him the sixth Bishop of Rochester.

N.C.W.C. News Service

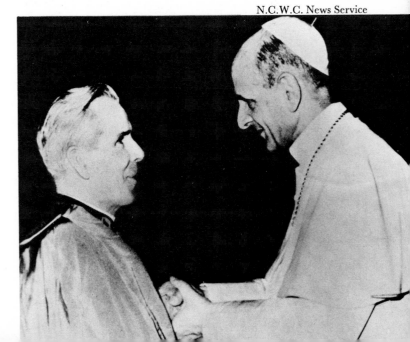

Senator Edward M. Kennedy escorts Sheen across the lawn of Hickory Hill, the late Senator Robert F. Kennedy's home in McLean, Virginia, on the occasion of the announcement of a ten million dollar foundation in memory of Robert of which Sheen is a member of the board of trustees.

Religious News Service

Sheen, aged 74, at the time of his resignation as Bishop of Rochester in 1969.

Religious News Service

United Press International

Sheen, as Bishop of Rochester, with his successor, Monsignor Joseph L. Hogan.

Religious News Service

Archbishop Sheen at "Honor America Day" ceremonies in Washington, D.C., 1970, with Rabbi Marc Tanenbaum and evangelist Billy Graham.

Archbishop Sheen in a typical role as the subject of an interview.

In his first television appearance since his retirement from the Diocese of Rochester, Archbishop Sheen tells Mike Wallace on "60 Minutes" that he could have risen higher in the Catholic hierarchy, but he "refused to pay the price."

Religious News Service

In every profession, in every walk of life, we have the charlatan and the phony, but to condemn all because of the mistakes of a few is irrational. There are many guilty people in the world. They need some sort of confession and forgiveness. There are, on the other hand, many sick people in the world, mentally ill, harassed with some crippling neurosis or psychosis, who need the attention of a psychiatrist. Sin and sickness are distinct. One does not necessarily cause the other.

Sheen, contrasting psychoanalysis and confession, said, "There is no morbidity in confession. You don't look so much on your sins, as you look upon your Savior who restores you to relationship with the Heavenly Father. Psychoanalysis gives no norms or standards. There are no more disintegrated people in the world than the victims of Freudian analysis. Confession gives you the standard of Christ—the perfect personality."

One has to distinguish between the will and the emotions. Confession deals with sin, the willful breaking of our relationship with God and our fellow men. Psychoanalysis deals with mental illness, with uncontrollable emotions. Dr. Lawrence, a well-known New York psychiatrist, challenged Sheen and asked him for a copy of his sermon. Sheen replied, "There are never any written copies of any of my sermons." The well-known New York psychiatrist Kulie asked for an appointment with Sheen to discuss the issue. He received no reply.

Kulie then wrote a letter to the *Herald Tribune* answer-

ing Sheen's charge that psychoanalysis is based on materialism, hedonism, infantilism, and eroticism. He stated that
"neither is its philosophy, purpose, or technique in psychoanalysis hedonistic, frivolous, or pleasure loving." Kulie
went on to say that Sheen completely misunderstood transference. It is not a transference of affection to the analyst,
but the incorporation of the analyst in the patient's fantasies
in a variety of symbolic roles. In the course of the therapy
the analyst becomes the object of "the entire gamut of
human feeling—hate, fear, rivalry, envy, feelings quite as
much as affection." Through the study of transference
phenomena, the patient can be given valuable insights into
the unconscious, psychological processes. And the study of
transference, Kulie said firmly, "is pursued quite as assidu-
ously if the patient is rich, or poor, or homely or beautiful."
Kulie pointed out the difference between feelings of guilt
and actual guilt. Psychoanalysis endeavors to eliminate
guilt feelings not rooted in reality. It does not seek to ab-
solve an individual of responsibility for his acts.

Dr. Frank J. Curran, a Catholic, resigned as chief psychiatrist at St. Vincent's Hospital in protest against the
failure of the New York chancery to disavow Sheen's remarks. In his letter of resignation, Curran said, "As a result
of the newspaper publicity given to Monsignor Sheen's
speech, private patients of mine, as well as hospital patients
at St. Vincent's, stated they could no longer come for
psychiatric treatment, or even consult a psychiatrist, because they would be committing a sin if they did."

In reply to Curran's letter, which was published, Sheen said that the *Times* had distorted his sermon. He quoted the first paragraph as follows: "I am not going to speak on psychiatry, which is a perfectly valid science, dealing with definite types of mental diseases. I am not speaking of psychoanalysis in general, which in its methods has rediscovered on its fringes the doctrine of Original Sin. I am speaking only of a particular type of psychoanalysis called Freudianism which is based on four assumptions—materialism, hedonism, infantilism, and eroticism—and this only to the extent that it denies sin and would supplant confession." Kulie said it was paradoxical that Sheen had no copy of the sermon, yet could quote the first paragraph. *The New York Times* stood behind the accuracy of the reporter.

In his book *Peace of Soul*, Sheen renewed the attack. He seems to have misunderstood Freud, who was rather an ascetic man. Sheen wrote: "Psychoanalysis never raises the question of the moral fitness of the analyst—as the Church does with her priests in the confessional." The American Medical Association will not certify a fledgling analyst if he is not found to be ethically and professionally responsible. Sheen continues: "Psychoanalysis based on a materialistic philosophy can offer no norms, no ideals, no motivation, no purpose in life. In a society with conflicting value systems it accepts the patients own norms or ideals, unless they are utterly unrealistic or plainly grounded in neurotic fantasies. No effort is made to convert an atheist or change the religion of the believer." Did Sheen alter his position on psychiatry, as he did on communism? Or did he sense psychiatry to be in vogue and adopt it?

While Sheen apparently did an about-face in his attitude toward peace of mind, he had great expertise in peace of soul. He was instrumental in bringing peace of soul to many well-known and unknown people. I remember Sheen often telling the following dramatic story. Douglas Hyde, who was the editor of the *Daily Worker*, the English Communist newspaper, and his wife were sitting down one evening listening to a radio talk on peace by Molotov. Suddenly Mrs. Hyde got up and turned off the radio. She said, "I don't believe Molotov believes in peace. He believes in war. I think his words of peace are loaded with bayonets." Douglas Hyde responded: "You are not talking like a good Communist. If you go on talking like this, I will report you to the party." She said, "Report me. I am going to get out of this hell I am living in." "Why?" he said, "you are talking like someone who is going to become a Catholic." She said, "I am." He stood up and said, "Shake hands. So am I."

Sheen at one time was not at all bashful about suggesting to people that they take instructions in the Catholic faith. He always looked about for prospective candidates, such as a person alongside him on a plane ride. Many a stewardess has an autographed book of the Bishop's, or a treasured rosary given her by him. Sheen used to give TWA a plug by quipping, "Travel With The Angels." When he journeyed on a train, or met someone by chance on the street, Sheen was always on duty for the Church. Since the time of Vatican Council II, however, things have changed; conversions to the Catholic Church have drastically diminished. The thrust of the Church today is Christian witness rather than proselytizing. Sheen here has been ahead of his time. For twenty years he has been advocating that the purpose of the missions is to feed the hungry and take care of the sick, and also give this Christian witness by a good life.

The return of Louis Budenz to the Catholic Church in 1945 got front-page coverage. His comeback came about in this way. Budenz wrote an article in the Communist *Daily Worker* attacking the Church. In answer, Sheen wrote a pamphlet, and to follow up, he called Budenz on the phone and invited him to lunch. "You name the restaurant, and I will pay the bill." He was interested to see if a Communist would choose a proletarian restaurant. He chose the Commodore. During the dinner, Budenz told Sheen: "I don't like you. You refuse to believe that communism is a democracy." Sheen said, "I am not going to discuss communism with you. I am going to talk to you about yourself." Budenz said, "You don't know anything about me." Sheen replied: "You would be surprised how much I know about you. You were an altar boy in Indianapolis." Their meeting ended. Years passed. Then Budenz wrote to Sheen and said he wanted to see him. Sheen replied that if he wanted to debate about communism, he was not interested. "If you want to see me about your soul, I am interested." Budenz wrote back, "I am willing to come back to the

and unpredictable. In the face of such a potential for massacre, destruction, and devastation, her puny efforts to alleviate human suffering and try to make a newer and better world seemed futile.

She resorted to psychiatry to seek answers to the riddle of life. "My heart had no light. I was still to struggle, to strive, to suffer, to sin, to betray, and to be betrayed, and to be unhappy. I was doomed to the psychic hell because I denied Freud. I demonstrated I had a free will. I could demonstrate my own path to hell."

Then there came that awful night in September 1945 in her room at the Waldorf Astoria, where she underwent pangs of hell. "I despaired of myself and for myself, and of the world, and for the world," she said. She was crying. She prayed the Our Father. When she finished she noticed an unopened letter from a Father Edward Wiatran, a Jesuit priest who had written to her about a speech she had made about war orphans. He wrote frequently to her. It was 2 A.M. She noticed the Church where he was staying, telephoned him and told him her problems. He said he was waiting for a call from her. "But I am not the one you should see. You must see Monsignor Fulton Sheen . . ."

Sheen recounts the meeting with Clare. "I invited Mrs. Luce to dinner in Washington. She brought up the subject of religion at dinner. I said it was better not to discuss religion at the table." After dinner, Sheen asked for about fifteen uninterrupted minutes of talk, and Clare could have the floor for two hours after this. Sheen was talking about five minutes when he mentioned the goodness of God. She bounded out of her seat, stuck a finger under his nose, and said, "Listen, if God is good, why did He take my daughter?"

Sheen answered, "In order that He might give you the greater blessing of drawing you to Himself which is beginning right now."

"Is that why you invited me?" she asked.

Sheen replied, "Certainly."

Clare's course of instruction lasted approximately five months. It was the longest Sheen had given. Usually from thirty to fifty hours were sufficient. Many of her friends argued against her entering the Church. However, on February 16, 1946, Sheen received her at a ceremony at St. Patrick's Cathedral in New York City. There were only six people present. A friend of Clare's, a non-Catholic, wrote: "Clare always had the capability of being great. There was her wonderful brain, her beauty, and her real desire to serve her country and all the peoples of the world. But there was something lacking. Her conversion to Catholicism had given her the humility, the gentleness, and the warmth to love individual people, as opposed to a sense of duty to humanity. These were the things she needed to make her the really great woman she is."

Of Sheen, Clare said, "I never knew a teacher who could be at once so patient and so unyielding, so poetical, so practical, so inventive, so orthodox. But rumor to the contrary, there is nothing particularly hypnotic about him.

What hypnotizes his converts is the sudden and unfamiliar sight of truth, and love, and the eternal which his instructions open to them. I have often been asked, 'Would you have become a Catholic, if you had not had Sheen to give you instructions?' My answer, 'Of course.' "

Clare was brilliant, yet often foolish; idealistic; yet realistic to the point of cynicism; tough as a Marine Sergeant, but almost paradoxically kind to unfortunates. She had the mind and courage of a man, yet possessed exceedingly feminine instincts. The complexities of her character are as numerous as the facets of her career: magazine editor, war correspondent, wit among wits, social reformer among starry-eyed liberals, playwright, congresswoman, ambassador to Italy, and wife of one of America's leading publishers.

Sheen and Clare are much alike—complex, opinionated, extremely talented individuals. Great talents bring great tensions. Genius has insights which the common man has not, but these insights bring added responsibilities. Both were tortured people; Clare found peace, Sheen has always been at war. Among his other converts have been Jews, a Moslem, a number of ministers, a well-known stockbroker, the world-famous opera star Grace Moore, and Jo Mielziner, who designed the settings for Sheen's TV program and for Michelangelo's "Pieta" at the World's Fair in New York.

At one time Sheen conducted convert classes in both New York and Washington, with as many as three to four hundred in each class. His conversion work slowed down when he moved to his East Thirty-eighth Street residence in New York, with possibly three or four a day. These people used to listen to about twenty-five hours instruction on tape, with about five hours of personal attention.

Sheen has written: "I believe on the last day God is going to ask priests, 'Where are your children?' God hates spiritual sterility. And when we come before Him for judgment, we will have to represent the soul we have saved. I'm only trying to save my soul. I know one way to do it, save others."

Another convert of Sheen's was Henry Ford II, a Methodist, who married Anne McDonnell, a member of one of New York's most prominent Irish Catholic families. Sheen said of Ford's conversion, "The inspiration was certainly Anne McDonnell. But Henry was a religious man in his own way. He often visited Church. Then it became known he was taking instructions. He came down from New Haven one day with the rear compartment of his car filled with mail. Everybody was telling him what a terrible thing he was doing."

On July 13, 1940, Anne and Henry were married by Sheen in the society wedding of the year. About twelve-hundred guests, and some seven-hundred and fifty spectators, including fifty prominent photographers, watched the newlyweds in Southampton, Long Island. They received almost a million dollars' worth of presents. Henry Ford I, then seventy-nine years old, overcame his anger at his son's marriage to a Catholic (He had toyed with the idea of disinheriting Henry II for marrying one.), and danced with the new Mrs. Ford. The union had the papal blessing of Pope Pius XII.

After twenty-three years of marriage to Anne McDonnell, and four years after a party at Maxims in Paris, at which he met Christina Austin, Henry and Anne received an uncontested divorce. A little more than a year later Henry and Christina were married. It was a quiet ceremony in the Ford Hotel suite in Washington with the judge who performed the ceremony and two witnesses. The announcement was not made until the next day. A representative of the Ford Company gave the announcement and a photo to the *Detroit News*—Ford had gratefully remembered the *News*'s restraint. A spokesman for the Archdiocese of Detroit annnounced that Ford remained a Catholic, but because of the laws of the Church on marriage, could not receive Holy Communion.

The conversion, too, of Heywood Broun made headlines in 1939. Some of his friends were shocked because he attacked Sheen's position on communism in his column. Sheen said of Broun, "Broun was known as a Commie—certainly as a friend of Commies." Sheen phoned Broun. "About your soul," said Sheen. "When?" "Next Friday at five." They met at a hotel in New York. Later on Sheen began instructing Broun, who loved humanity, who really loved human beings. Sheen gave him his First Communion and he was the first person to be confirmed by Spellman when the man from Boston arrived in New York to take over as Archbishop. Not long after, Broun became ill and died. Sheen preached his eulogy at St. Patrick's Cathedral. Here again there was the man and the myth: the man, Sheen, a really excellent instructor; the myth, that he alone had the keys to the kingdom.

CHAPTER

8

NOT A MYTH, ONLY A MAN

WHEN Sheen was national director of the Society for the Propagation of the Faith in New York, a copy of this poem by Charles Mackay hung on the wall of his office:

> You have no enemies you say,
> Alas, my friend, the boast is poor
> He who has mingled in the fray
> of duty must have made foes.
> If you have none
> Small is the work you have done.
> You've hit no traitor on the hip
> You've dashed no cup from perjured lip
> You've never turned wrong to right
> You've been a coward in the fight.

Sheen can be charming, sympathetic, brilliant, beguiling, entertaining, and companionable; also reserved, private, extremely opinionated, and unable really to reveal himself to anybody.

Sheen is far more human than his portrait indicates. While endowed with extraordinary talents and having been showered with superhuman adulation, he still remains a human being. He is a restless, driven man who sleeps little and eats little. Behind the legend there is a complicated man. He does not smoke or drink; however, he is no ascetic.

His preaching of poverty and the way he lived were again contradictory. As we have seen, when he was in Washington, he lived in a very expensive home. He had a fine Cadillac supplied each year. His suits, shoes, and shirts were especially made to measure for him. In New York City, he was chauffeur driven by his Italian driver Mario. This worldliness is half the story. His former boss, a C.U. Fr. Ignatius Smith, said of Sheen: "He was always a very holy man. You could tell that in a minute. Kneeling before the Blessed Sacrament for an hour every day is not at all required but Sheen did it and there was no parade or ostentation about it."

Sheen seems to be in an endless tormented dialogue between his demanding urges for personal success and the sense of guilt that ran side by side with it. That is why he was not a good administrator: he personalized his work too much. Sheen goes through the words when he delights in his wordly triumphs and when he feels the fervor of religious agony. He runs all the gamut of the emotions.

Sheen has been compared to Churchill, who saw the rise of nazism but whose warnings went unheeded. A Europe raped and razed to the ground was the outcome. He predicted the rise of communism and the danger of Soviet

Russia infiltrating the bloodstream of the world in post-World War II Europe. His prediction went unnoticed. As we know, there have been outstanding orators, outstanding leaders, and outstanding statesmen. It is quite common for a public figure to be one of the three at the expense of the other two. Winston Churchill was a man who was all three. As an orator, Sheen was as good as, if not better than, Churchill.

Churchill differed from Sheen in one respect—he was a great politician. Sheen never had the stomach or the time for the infighting and backroom antics of politics, and probably because of this he never reached the top, perhaps to his credit. He was not at ease in the behind-the-scenes interplay of people and thus he found his calvary in Rochester.

Sheen and Churchill were both saturated in the nobility and profundity of Shakespeare. Both could recite long passages from memory. Both in a sense saw themselves in the roles of some of Shakespeare's famous characters, and like General Patton, relived history and saw themselves in it. When the history of the Twentieth Century is written, men like Gandhi, Churchill, MacArthur, Hammarskjold, King, Kennedy, and De Gaulle will rate highest in its pages. The Church never gave Sheen the real opportunity to test his metal. Would he have been among those outstanding men? Now we will never know.

Sheen is about five feet eight inches tall, though he looked taller on TV. He has a large shock of thick gray hair.

Sheen really emotes and in his presence one feels a flow of psychic energy. His deep-set eyes are powerful and were especially so on TV—in a close-up those blue eyes can mesmerize a man for a while. Some people thought his policies were unduly influenced by his personal secretary— Edith Brownett. She was in charge of his appointments and at times the right people did not get through to him at the right time.

Sheen is not a typical American. He never was a forty-hour-a-week man. Those who have been overawed by his charm and personality when they have seen him on TV, or have met him in person, will find it difficult to believe how dull a social life he has led. His recreation used to be tennis twice a week. He claimed he was not old enough to play golf. He did not watch much TV, except the news or an occasional baseball or football game. The late Fritz Kreisler persuaded Sheen to take organ lessons, and he is a fair organist. Sheen, strictly speaking, never took a vacation. His idea of one was to go some place where it was quiet and there was a big library. As someone once commented, "Sheen only spoils his food."

While in New York, Sheen used to ride a special black Checker Cab. There was no meter for fares. He explains that Checker taxicabs are the only motorcars which permit one to climb into the back seat without being either a pretzel or an acrobat. Sheen used to say it might have been a good idea to have kept the light on the roof flashing a sign: "Sacrifice for the poor in the missions."

Every man in his time plays many parts. Sheen is certainly an enigma. At the Society for the Propagation of the Faith in New York, he was the sympathetic counselor, the humble cleric, the thundering Savonarola of the airwaves, the man of fashion who drove around in a Cadillac as well as the Checker Cab, and the tennis player at the exclusive River Club. In Rochester he was trying to be the epitome of a modern-day bishop, championing the minority groups, fraternizing with the peoples of all faiths and of none, or a kind of den mother of the New Left. Then he resigned as dramatically as he entered the upstate diocese.

When Sheen first came to New York to take over as head of the Society for the Propagation of the Faith, he lived where he worked, at 109 East Thirty-eighth Street. Two priest assistants lived with him. His staff at that time numbered about thirty. Then he moved the Propagation offices to fashionable 366 Fifth Avenue, near the Empire State Building. His day used to begin at 6 A.M. He spent a "Holy Hour" of meditation and preparation for mass at 8 A.M., which he celebrated in his private chapel. He was supposed to have seven hours' sleep but most nights he would spend some of that time reading. From 9 to 10 A.M. he used to write, finishing some article he was working on or continuing some book for which he had a deadline to meet for the publishers. From 10 to 12 he would work on his mail, which came to him from all corners of the globe. His lunches were work ones. Missionaries from all over the world who passed through New York used to stop in and see him, and he invited them to lunch. A priest from Brazil, a missionary bishop from Africa, a French foreign missionary from Korea made lunch with him a veritable United Nations. They kept him abreast of foreign affairs. From 2 to 6 again Sheen had his appointments with various people. At 6 he dined again but rarely ate much; a corner of steak, a lamb chop, and some vegetables. After supper it was study, reading of new books, study again—certainly an unglamorous sort of existence.

All that changed in Rochester. He had to be out among the people and visiting his priests, leaving him little time to study. He tried hard at this; perhaps it was too late. Sheen in his day accomplished ten times as much work as any businessman on Madison Avenue. He was no cloistered mystic. He was a creative writer, editor, TV star, public relations man, fund-raiser, a bishop in the spirit of Vatican Council II.

A friend of Sheen's is Ed Sullivan, who himself has become a TV Institution. Ed is married to a beautiful Jewish woman. Some years ago the sardonic Ed had a serious operation. Sheen went to visit him, and Sullivan's wife claims it was the turning point for the good in Sullivan's recovery. Sheen has been a guest on all the TV talk shows. He has appeared with the smiling choirboy from California, Merv Griffin, who with Johnny Carson and Dick Cavett must be the co-chairmen of the insomaniacs of America. Sheen has appeared also on the two latter shows. One of his most interesting talk-show appearances was when the Microphone of God, Sheen, was on with the Microphone of Great Britain, David Frost.

Down through the years too Sheen has been a friend, confidant, and spiritual adviser to Jackie Gleason. Jackie too is a many-faceted man; comic, straight actor, composer, philosopher. Jackie at one time made a study of all the great religions. He confesses he is not the best Catholic in the world, but that he is on the right team. He has been up and down too many times to believe in the permanence of success, but his ego has remained intact. For years Gleason has relied on Sheen for encouragement and advice. They have much in common. When Gleason did a tribute to the slain President Kennedy on his Christmas program of 1963, it was written by Sheen.

Sheen had a great variety of friends. When the late President Eisenhower was in the White House, he had six series of brain-trust stag dinners. To one of these dinners Sheen was invited. In the thirties a great friend of Sheen's was Irish-born Maureen O'Sullivan, also known as the mother of Mia Farrow, who once was married to Frank Sinatra. Sheen has been for some time a personal friend of predominantly Catholic Belgium's King Baudoin and his wife.

Another friend of Sheen's is the world-famous portrait artist, Armenian-born Yousuf Karsh, whose famous portrait of Winston Churchill in 1941 rocketed him to fame. Karsh's first wife died and he was remarried to Estrellita Nachbar in Our Lady's Chapel in St. Patrick's Cathedral in New York.

Sheen performed the ceremony. Karsh did the beautiful photographic work on four very successful works of Sheen's: *This is Rome, This is the Mass, Holy Land, These are the Sacraments.* Another close friend of Sheen's is Salvador Dali. Sheen used Dali's "Christ of St. John of the Cross" as the cover for his best-selling work, *The Life of Christ.*

In the famous Quentin Reynolds versus Westbrook Pegler libel case, the renowned lawyer Louis Nizer was Reynolds' counsel. Nizer contemplated calling Fulton Sheen as witness, since it was he who had converted Heywood Broun to Catholicism. At Heywood's funeral, Sheen had ridden together with Connie Broun and Reynolds to the cemetery. Sheen was an eyewitness and could give conclusive evidence that Reynolds had not proposed to Mrs. Broun on the way to the cemetery from her husband's funeral, as alleged by Pegler. Sheen and Nizer were close friends. They had introduced each other at various banquets and functions. Out of respect for Sheen, Nizer if at all possible did not want to call him as a witness. Pegler produced a Catholic priest as a witness. Nizer as a result of this advised Sheen he might have to call him as a rebuttal witness. Sheen replied; "I will of course do my duty, Louis, but I still plead with you not to involve me in this unpleasant lawsuit if you can possibly help it." Sheen was grateful that Nizer never felt it necessary to call on him.

Sheen gave the invocation at the swearing-in ceremony for Mayor Lindsay's first term as mayor of "Fun City."

Sheen has such other diverse friends as former Postmaster
General James Farley, columnists Bob Considine and Jack
O'Brian, and the man of many moods, Jack Paar.

Sheen's emotions made him more open to the new moment. He was best when he relied on his instincts instead
of his reason. When he intellectualized about a problem he
usually followed the party line of the institutional Church.
He was more authentic when he followed the dictates of
his own passions. Sheen has mingled in the fray; he has
made many friends, he has turned many wrongs to right, he
has not been a coward in the fight.

Down through the years one of the voices raised against
the evils of society has been that of Fulton Sheen. Another
voice has been that of Billy Graham, who once admitted
borrowing some of Sheen's ideas and expressions. (I once
saw a catchy poster that read: "God is not dead—Billy
Graham," and underneath it: "Who the Hell is Billy
Graham?—God.") Graham has been a friend of presidents—
he is particularly close to Richard Nixon who apparently
has made him a kind of unofficial White House chaplain.
Graham is a fundamentalist. He studies the Bible intently—
has actually worn out about ten copies of the King James
Version. Graham has not the intelligence or indeed the
flamboyance of Sheen, but he is a very sincere man.

It is inevitable that Sheen should be compared to some of
these more articulate voices of radio and television. In the
late fifties, James Pike had a Sunday night TV show on
ABC with a large audience. Many watched him because he

was extremely controversial. When he was consecrated bishop in the Spring of 1958, he was publicly advised by a clerical friend to engage in controversy as a last and not a first resort. From the pulpit of what was called the "Dean Pike Show," he tangled with the late Cardinal Spellman on movie censorship. He attacked Senator Joseph McCarthy and battled for birth control, dubbing the rhythm method "Vatican Roulette." He did not have the suavity, the intellectuality, or the finesse of Sheen—on the other hand, he was appallingly honest. His term as Episcopal Bishop of California was a stormy one. His attack on Lucie Johnson's conditional baptism on her reception into the Catholic Church caused an international furor. His having Martin Luther King preach in Grace Cathedral in San Francisco and his marching on the dusty, sun-drenched roads of Alabama for civil rights cost him the support of his more sober affluent flock. Pike never had the following that Sheen had on TV. Sheen was more dramatic, more of an orator, more poetic, Pike spoke in the hard prose of daily living, attacking many of the so-called sacred institutions. He was a kind of national examination of conscience. He was a lot like Sheen—restless—a misunderstood and tortured man. He met his death under unfortunate circumstances in the Holy Land, looking for the peace of soul and the truth he desperately sought all his life.

Another successful TV religious personality was Dr. Norman Vincent Peale, of whom the late great Adlai Stevenson commented, "I find Paul appealing and Peale appalling." Peale limited Christianity, however, to personal problems. His program was called "The Art of Living." He was highly repetitive, a rather poor storyteller, and a trifle superficial. He certainly did not possess the academic background of Sheen, whose charm, humor, presentation, and golden voice are difficult to equal. Peale's program was not theological in content. Rather he was giving psychological answers to middle-class problems. Of course the twentieth-century world and mind have been obsessed with the fears and worries to which Peale spoke. Ours is a neurotic society. Whoever speaks a comfortable word to such an age will get a hearing, especially if the words are simple and entirely devoid of barbs and nettles. Peale appealed to middle-class America. During the 1960 election campaign he took the side of his friend Richard Nixon. Sheen was silent. Peale said of the election, "Our American culture is at stake. I don't say it won't survive [if Kennedy were elected] but it won't be what it was." This remark of Peale's exhibited much religious intolerance, and his attitude stirred a wave of anger and dismay from coast to coast.

Sheen's frequent brief allusions in his telecasts to philosophers, books, and abstract concepts gave tremendous prestige to his program. Sheen's program was unique in that he was on the air at prime time and his so-called religious program could hold its own with the television greats.

Sheen provided his audiences with something they could use on many different levels of meaning: to the uneducated who felt their lack, Sheen was understanding, the superbly

educated man who could lift them toward his level; to the
timid he was a resolute symbol of masculine competence
and assurance; to the people of all faiths, and of none,
Sheen was not preaching Roman Catholicism but simple
goodness; to the crackpots and bigots, of whom there are
many, indeed too many, Sheen was a scapegoat on whom to
vent their hostility; to the people of no faith he was the
father figure, the handsome, dynamic, he-man directing
their lives. He fulfilled the demands of the gamut of human
emotions, making life worth living for countless millions.

Sheen was introduced by a musical theme at the beginning of each program. He used to stride with vigorous purpose to the center of the set, vested in his bishop's robes.
He faced the studio audience, which also put him full face
to the TV cameras. He relied upon camera movement to
give the TV audience a sense of intimate contact with him.
His piercing eyes seemed to penetrate the very souls of his
audience. He was a compelling, dynamic speaker who was
able to employ a variety of vocal ranges, facial expressions,
and gestures.

CHAPTER
9

IT'S THE IRISH: SHEEN
AND THE BROTHERS KENNEDY

APRIL 20, 1952, was a really big day in the village of Croghan in North Roscommon, Ireland, when Bishop Fulton Sheen came back to the place where his grandmother was born to dedicate the 350-year-old rebuilt parish Church of St. Michael. Not only the village, but farms in the countryside were decorated for the occasion. Irish tri-colors were flown with the Stars and Stripes and the papal flag. The little church, which holds about six hundred people, was completely filled, with a big overflow crowd outside, when Bishop Sheen, accompanied by a large group of clergy, began the impressive ceremony of dedication, followed by a pontifical high mass. At night people came to the village by the thousands from all parts of Ireland to hear Bishop Sheen preach at the evening service. Loudspeakers carried his voice outside to the great numbers filling the village streets.

The occasion brought back memories of the Eucharistic Congress of 1932, where he gave an address. He remembered the mass, which half a million attended, and the "Panis Angelicus" ringing out over the cool Dublin air, sung by the late great John McCormack. In this talk Sheen recited the beautiful poem of Joseph Mary Plunkett:

I see His blood upon the rose
And in the stars the glory of His eyes
His body gleams amid eternal snows
His tears fall from the skies.
I see his face in every flower
The thunder and the singing of the birds
Are but his voice.
And carven by his power, rocks are his written words
All pathways by His feet are worn
His strong heart stirs the ever-beating sea
His crown of thorns is chained with every thorn
His cross is every tree.

When Sheen came to the line, "I see His face in every flower," his mind went blank. He recalled the advice of a famous writer who said, "If you are in trouble in a speech, throw yourself into the middle of the next sentence, and trust to God Almighty to get you to the other end." Sheen began: "I have forgotten—I am glad I have forgotten because standing on the soil of Ireland, one should be able to hammer and forge one's own poetry, and not be dependent on a magnanimous someone like Joseph Mary Plunkett." The Archbishop of Dublin, who presided, said:

"Father Sheen, that was a marvelous trick of oratory—pretending you forgot."

When you mention the name "Ireland," what ideas come to mind? Pints of Guinness Stout, the late Brendan Behan—all lit up, "When Irish Eyes Are Smiling," the gusty young civil rights leader Bernadette Devlin, the bigoted Paisley, Sweepstakes tickets, rosary beads, late marriages, politics, ballad singing, and yes, rain—plenty of rain? But Ireland is known for more than that: it has provided great Churchmen, orators, and politicians. Irish priests, sisters, and brothers, laymen and laywomen are scattered throughout the world as missionaries. In 1961 they celebrated in Ireland the 1500th Anniversary of the death of the great missionary to the Irish, St. Patrick. There was a week of festivities. The close of the congress called Patrician was attended by the Papal Legate Cardinal Agagianian and many other dignitaries. The final talk of the congress was given by Fulton J. Sheen. He said he was glad to be in Ireland, as his grandparents did not come from Bessarabia. He remarked that St. Patrick installed a Divine restlessness in the Irish, that the Irish had a great sense of humor, and made the world a better and happier place in which to live. On Judgment Day, he predicted, God would manifest Himself in various ways to the different nations: to the Italians, Spanish, and Germans, who love pomp, He would show Himself as the King of Kings; to the Asiatics, who waited so long for the coming of Christ, He would show Himself in the brilliance of His eyes; but to the Irish, who have made it a happy world, He would show them something He showed to no other people. He would show them His smile. Sheen certainly stole the hearts of the Irish that night and made them feel taller. However, I am sure that Sheen recognizes that his poetic analysis of the Irish is not the same as the prose of daily living. I am sure he knows, too, that Irish Catholicism, lay and clerical, has no special mandate from God, and no guarantee of its future in the soul-searching pilgrimage that is the unique path of the Universal Church in the exciting, but very different and difficult, last third of the Twentieth Century.

At a banquet once held in Washington for Ireland's best-known statesman, President Eamon De Valera, Sheen remarked there were three eras in Irish history, the Pagan era, the Christian era, and the De Valera. To which the President replied that some would like to call his era "The Devil's Era."

Sheen in no small way helped to create an atmosphere in the United States in which a Catholic, indeed an Irish Catholic, could occupy the White House. By his TV program, he did a great deal to kill bigotry and create an atmosphere of tolerance and an era of good will. He showed that the Irish have class, that the Catholic Church is not void of intellectuals, and that both can be part of the mainstream of the American way of life.

The late President Kennedy once said, "Three things in life are real: God, human feeling, and laughter. The first two are beyond our comprehension, so we do what we can with the third." In the office of the late President was a picture of a small boat on the ocean with the following inscription: "O, God, your sea is so great and my boat is so small." This represents the pathos of the Irish as Sheen aptly puts it: laughter and tears in Ireland, it rains through the sunshine and makes rainbows.

The effect of President Kennedy's trip to Ireland was electrifying. There were no divided opinions about him in the Emerald Isle. On leaving he promised, like the poet, "to come back in the springtime and see Shannon's face once more." But he was unfortunately cut down by a sniper's bullet under a hot Dallas sun—and we were orphans.

Sheen said this of President Kennedy's death:

Only twice perhaps in the history of our nation has the desire to unite men in peace made Presidents take on themselves the burden of human inequality to the point of saving others at the cost of self. On a bright Easter Day, we shall see that our national Brotherhood was purchased by the blood of a victim —John Fitzgerald Kennedy. In the future, too—at the other end of a pool where the image of the victim Lincoln is reflected—there will be cast another monument, the heroic image of the victim Kennedy—for both were great, not by what was done by them, but what was done through them. He has crossed the "new Frontier," that mysterious dividing line where a man goes to render an account of his stewardship. He need not fear—for blessed are those who suffer in the cause of right. Lincoln's death gave us peace for decades afterwards. May God grant through the same Calvary law of sacrifice in President Kennedy that peace which the world cannot give. Above all our national heroes these two Presidents of sorrow stand forever near the man of sorrow, saying, "I will stand here at Thy side. Despise my nation not."

We were beginning to laugh again, then Martin Luther King was taken from us, and two months later Robert Kennedy was killed reaching out to shake hands with a $75-a-week Mexican dishwasher in a downtown Los Angeles hotel.

Bishop Sheen knelt at the coffin of Robert Kennedy in St. Patrick's Cathedral in New York, to pray for him—then changed his mind and prayed for the United States. A friend of the Senator's, Sheen explained why he decided to pray for the nation rather than for the Senator. "His death," he said, "is an expiation for any life. He's in his glory. So I found my prayers instead were for our country. There's too much red in our American flag—too much fire—too much passion, bloodshed, and hate. We've forgotten about the blue which symbolizes loyalty, and the white that symbolizes innocence and decency." Referring to the assassinations of John F. Kennedy and Martin Luther King, Sheen continued, "The great shocks may now make us more conscious of the emptiness of our affluence and make us begin to love one another and stop this hate." He paused and added: "But why does it take death to pull us together?"

In June of 1964, in a personally written speech, Robert Kennedy made these remarks at the Free University of West Berlin, which summed up his inmost feelings.

There were many who felt that the torchbearer for a whole generation was gone . . . that an era was over before its time . . . But I have come to understand that the hope President Kennedy enkindled is not dead, but alive . . . The torch still burns, and because it does, there remains for all of us a chance to light up the tomorrows and brighten the future. For me, this is the challenge that makes life worthwhile.

Sheen and the Brothers Kennedy—each in his own way—has made "Life Worth Living" for countless millions at home and in our global village.

In a telecast in December of 1966 Sheen gave a talk on what he called four modern day saints: Gandhi, Pope John, Dag Hammarksjold, and John F. Kennedy. Sheen spoke of having read five or six books on the late President Kennedy, none of which really described the very core of the man. Sheen said it was the occult cross of which Kennedy never spoke. Half his adult life he was in continuous pain. On August 2, 1943, Kennedy was in command of P.T. Boat 109 in the Pacific. A Japanese destroyer cut it in two. Kennedy was in the water for thirteen hours. During those trying times he realized what it was to face death. As a result of that accident, he had a back injury which necessitated two operations. He was twice given the last rites of his Church. Pain can be a great purifier. Kennedy learned knowledge from books, but wisdom from suffering, which gave him the great compassion he had.

In the strict sense, John F. Kennedy would not have been termed a fervent Catholic. He had spent only one year in a Catholic school. Kennedy once said, "There is an old saying in Boston that we get our religion from Rome and our politics at home, and that is the way most Catholics feel about it."

In 1960, while running for the Presidency, Kennedy made a historic speech in Houston, Texas, on Church-State affairs. There were several hundred ministers present. He said:

I believe in an America where the separation of Church and State is absolute—where no Catholic Prelate would tell the President (should he be Catholic) how to act, and no Protestant Minister would tell his parishioners for whom to vote—where no Church or Church school is granted any public funds or political preference—and where no man is denied public office merely because his religion differs from the President who might appoint him or the people who might elect him. Many believed this was the turning point in the campaign.

Kennedy saw no dichotomy between these beliefs and the culture religion of America. Kennedy as a culture hero laid the groundwork for the forces of encounter within American Catholicism. He opened the minds of non-Catholics to new opportunities for dialogue by showing that whether one is Catholic, Protestant, or Jew, or a man of good will, God's work on this earth must truly be ours.

After the congressional elections of November 1970, a youth in Boston carried a sign which read "Our Father who art in Congress." The Reverend Representative was Father

Robert F. Drinan, former Dean of Boston College Law School, a Roman Catholic priest, a Jesuit. He is the first priest to be popularly elected to represent a district in Congress. One other Catholic priest, The Reverend Gabriel Richard, served in that body in 1842 as a selected delegate from the territory of Michigan.

With the election of Drinan, a new form of priesthood has begun—the priest-politician. Surprisingly enough, the greatest opposition to his election came from the Catholics in his constituency, the collar being a hindrance rather than a help. It is a coincidence that Drinan was elected from Boston. It was a man from Boston, John F. Kennedy, who broke the religious barrier by being the first Roman Catholic to become President. Drinan's election marked the dawning of a new era of priests becoming more involved in the political arena where the real power is. Sheen was never really involved politically, but as a great communicator, he had a tremendous influence on the changing role of Catholics in the political scene, despite his lack of direct involvement.

Within a few years after Kennedy's election, Catholicism in America got a new lease on life. Kennedy was the complete opposite to the stereotyped Catholic, who is parochial, anti-intellectual, suspicious, tribalistic, and ruled by fear rather than love. To Kennedy the Church was meant to be a source of freedom and self-liberation. Kennedy was America's counterpart of another of Sheen's modern Saints, Sweden's Dag Hammarskjold.

Hammarskjold was described by Pope Pius XII as "a lay Pope." The statesman was an example of the prevalence of the positive virtues over the negative ones. He was a citizen of the world and became involved in all the issues of our global village. He once said, "In our era, the road to holiness necessarily passes through the world of action." Hammarskjold's diaries are the X-rays of a human soul. They present to modern man a challenge to grapple with present-day conflicts in this technocratic and scientific age—man must now know not only the how, but the why. The acceptance of that transcendence which many call God brings an inner core of strength and peace. Hammarskjold never married— here was the true celibate; he lived completely for others.

Kennedy was a catalyst of change among Catholics in America. Pope John XXIII, with his two encyclicals, *Mater e Magistra* and *Pacem in Terris*, and the calling of Vatican Council II, broke down the walls of Catholic separatism in America, as well as in many places throughout the world. Increasingly helpful too was the penetrating self-criticism of a Kung, a De Lubac, a Congar, a Rahner, and the extremely influential work of the French Jesuit paleontologist, Teilhard de Chardin.

John F. Kennedy, unconsciously and unknowingly, was an example of the incarnational theology, involvement in the world, advocated by De Chardin, who died in New York City in the 1950's. Two of his books, *The Phenomena of Man* and *Divine Milieu*, both published posthumously, were best sellers. The Vatican forbade Chardin to publish any of his works while he was alive.

One of the great achievements of Chardin was to create a living dialogue between science and religion. He was a forerunner of Vatican Council II and the Aggiornamento, the new spring envisioned by Pope John.

Robert Kennedy often wondered why the graduates of Catholic schools were so conservative, so parochial in outlook, and not really dedicated to the great issues of our time. While John Kennedy was the intellectual, Robert was the activist. He was morally conservative, a little puritanical in his own religious life. He was, however, always rooting for the underdog; the Mexican-American, the neglected Indian, the blacks in the ghetto, the Puerto Ricans, and the poor whites. He learned from the people rather than from books. Always reverent toward priests, he nevertheless showed how he felt about those with whom he disagreed vehemently.

When one sees the quality of some of our leaders in the state and in the Church today, one wishes for the guidance of those who went before them. We are grateful for their memory. A man like Al Smith led the way for a Catholic reaching the White House. A man like Fulton Sheen contributed immensely. In his time he was the only see-and-hear member of his Church known to millions of Americans. He was a noble champion of his own Church; he was also an intelligent open man who in his own way created an atmosphere of acceptance and openness, in which a Catholic—indeed an Irish Catholic—could have as an address 1600 Pennsylvania Avenue. For this we must be grateful to Sheen and the brothers Kennedy.

CHAPTER

10

WHERE IS LOVE?

AT A birthday party for Jackie Gleason in Miami, Fulton Sheen was standing in the wings to go on to pay tribute to the guest of honor. As Sheen waited nervously, scantily clad members of the June Taylor dancing group bustled by him. A TV cameraman, a devout Catholic, timidly approached Sheen, and inquired, "Your Excellency, aren't you embarrassed to be among all these pretty dancers?" Sheen, never at a loss for words, smiled broadly and quipped, "No. Even though I am on a diet, I can still look at the menu."

Many priests, however, not only look at the menu, they choose from it as well. Clerical celibacy is one of the most burning issues in the Catholic Church today. Should priests be allowed to marry and carry on their ministry?

David Frost, interviewing Sheen, queried: "Do you ever regret never knowing the love of a woman in fact?"

Sheen replied: "No, no, no. Because, after all, remember, one is not to think one is without love. This would be a great mistake. There are higher loves, and if that did not exist, celibacy would be impossible. And just as soon as one falls away from that higher love, celibacy does become increasingly difficult."

In his book *The World's First Love* Sheen writes: "A man is normally more serene than a woman, more absorbent of the daily shocks of life, less distributed by trifles, but on the other hand, in the great crises of life, it is the woman who, because of her gentle power of reigning, can give great consolation to man in his troubles. When he is remorseful, sad and disquieted, she brings comfort and assurance. As the surface of the ocean is agitated and troubled, but the great depths are calm, so in the really great catastrophes which affect the soul, the woman is the depth, and the man the surface."

Mike Wallace once remarked to Sheen during an interview: "Of course, a good many priests are today no longer interested in remaining celibate. They want to marry."

Sheen's comment was: "That's a very normal desire. Celibacy is not an easy thing. Celibacy is a gift; it is not something which the Church asks. In the Gospel our Blessed Lord described it as a gift, and he said, 'Let those who will take this gift, take it.' And it is always hard; it is always a wrestling, and there will be some who stumble. But people are divided into two classes—there are the pigs, and there are the sheep. Pigs fall into the mud and stay there; sheep fall into the mud and they get out. They wrestle with the problem."

This last observation by Sheen was an unhappy one. He seemed to be referring to priests who have left the active ministry as pigs. His penchant for summarizing serious problems with catchy phrases once more caused much hurt. These words were soon to be quoted in a way that rubbed at already open sores in the Roman Catholic Church.

The attitude of the Church toward women has been faulty. After all, they make up half the human race, and they were created by God. When a priest recounts a crisis of faith to any Vatican official, the question in reply usually is, "What is her name?"

All men have mothers—cardinals and bishops and priests, and even the Pope himself. The Church should look at women as persons, helping them to be themselves and free, not vessels for men's pleasure, but companions, helpmates, standing shoulder to shoulder with men, facing the problems of life, and celebrating the joy in the unfolding mystery of the world. Many today feel that celibacy should be a free choice, freely taken. For some, celibacy is their rule in life; for others, salvation may come through marriage. A day will come when priests will be allowed to be married, and when, indeed, the respected married men in the community may become priests.

The celibate life should not be deemed better than the married life. They both have their agonies and ecstasies. A lady in her early thirties asked a priest at a parish meeting, "Do you think the Pope will ever allow yourself to marry?" The young priest quipped, "We won't, but our sons will."

Yearly, about seven thousand nuns leave their order, and about ten thousand priests request dispensation from the vow of celibacy. The urgency of the problem was highlighted by the marriage of Monsignor Musante, one of Pope Paul's close aides. Celibacy has to be lived to the full if it is to be a sign. The jet-set priest with the gold cuff links, and the maxi bank account, and the mini brain, the supermarket sacrament-giver, who likes his horses young and fast, and his scotch old, is hardly a sign of Christ in a struggling community.

In their spring meeting of 1971 the American bishops went on record as adamant backers of the celibacy law, despite growing opposition from their priests. A study undertaken under the bishops' aegis also pointed out the need for a change in the law. This recalcitrance further polarized the American Church.

Women never really came of age in the Church. They have been guided solely by men. But since Vatican Council II, the nuns are on the march. The convent doors have been thrown open. They are emerging into the world, wanting desperately to be part of the human scene, fulfilling their personalities.

The new nun is a visionary. She is creating the Church community of the future, and many have even "kicked the habit." Corita Kent, the gifted artist, and Jacqueline Grennon, the influential educator, have left their orders. In their time they were two of America's best-known nuns.

All during his life, Sheen emphasized that the purpose of the Church is personal discovery, rather than a blind obedience to sterile laws and moralistic traditions. More and more each day, nuns are finding work outside the institutional Church as doctors, social workers, nurses, and teachers in the public schools. They are fulfilling the function of the Church, whose purpose is to serve people, not to build up the institution.

Celibacy, however, is not the fundamental problem of the priesthood. The real problem is the crisis of identity. Birth control, divorce, and antiquated parochial school systems, a malignant neglect of the urban poor, the emphasis of legalism over love, the indifference to the race question, the Church's failure to take a firm, clear stand on war and peace—these are the great issues, the gut issues that eat away at the heart of the average priest. From all sides he is thwarted in doing a humane job.

Cardinal John Wright, the Vatican's top authority on the clergy, once told a Roman audience that priests who want to marry and work are immature. He told the story of a woman who dragged into Wright's office her husband, a priest who requested to be reduced to lay state, after his marriage outside the Church. "In God's name," the woman asked, "why did you ordain that?" Wright quoted her as explaining, "Two weeks after we were married I discovered I had not married a man, I had adopted a small boy. I think I love him, but I pity him more. I think it'll take about two years to make a man out of him, and then kick him out." Wright said that the woman asked him not to grant lay status to her husband, because if he granted it, "I might have to marry him in the Church, and then I'd be stuck." The Cardinal said, "As for priests who ask to be reduced to the lay state, I don't know the meaning of the word." He continued, "It's like resigning from the human race. To whom do you send the letter?"

There is a cartoon of a young girl introducing her boyfriend to her parents over cocktails and saying, "Quite frankly the first time I saw John saying the 12 noon Mass, I said to myself—'That's the man for me.'" To Pope Paul VI celibacy is a "crowning jewel" of the Roman Catholic Church. On the other hand, to many priests it is a crown of thorns.

James P. Shannon, the former Auxiliary Bishop of Minneapolis, Minnesota, was ordained to that office by Cardinal Egidio Vagnozzi. He was then the Vatican's Apostolic Delegate to the United States. At that time Vagnozzi observed: "They criticize us for not having intellectuals in the hierarchy—now we have an intellectual and we shall see what happens."

When James Shannon said, "I do—I do" to the thrice-married Ruth Wilkinson, he became the first Roman Catholic bishop in the United States to break Church law by taking to himself a wife. Shannon was the liberal spokesman within the American hierarchy. He was the only Catholic bishop to have marched side by side with Martin Luther King in Selma. He was also a dove in regard to Vietnam and participated in peace marches. When Pope Paul VI issued his encyclical letter on birth control, Shannon wrote a private letter to the Holy Father pointing out that he could not in conscience accept his teaching.

Shannon's marriage was the culmination of a frustrating career as a bishop. His colleagues who applauded his progressive stance in private let him stand alone when he was stumbling under ecclesiastical pressure. Apparently the former Archbishop of Los Angeles, Cardinal McIntyre, would not accept Shannon's views and prevented him from getting a Church promotion. We will never have unity in the Church until pluriformity is tolerated.

The great dropout among priests is popularly attributed to celibacy. But the opinion was shattered recently by a Jesuit priest-sociologist, Eugene Schallert of San Francisco. In a sociological study he pointed out his findings that the desire to marry had little to do with priests leaving, and surprisingly the age of clerical dropouts is going up rather than down.

Father Schallert had had various audiences with Pope Paul to discuss the present crisis in the priesthood. The Vatican Council, according to Schallert, had produced a new breed of priest who no longer views the Church in competition with the world. This new priest is more interested in rapid change than stifling stability. He views himself as an individual and not a cog in the clerical machine. Vatican Council II affirmed the priest's dignity as a human being and places this dignity in his power "to think and be free."

The dropout problem occurs, according to Schallert, "when a bishop or superior tells a priest all he has to do is say his prayers and all his problems will be all right." Schallert's studies indicate that those priests leaving are in

the top quarter of the priesthood in qualities such as creativity, charisma, freedom. He finds that most of them really
remain committed to the Church—they look upon dropping
out as a meaningful religious value.

Almost all priests, according to Schallert, can handle
celibacy. He says: "Women become significant in the life
of a Catholic priest only after he has made at least a latent
decision to leave the clergy." In other words, priests tend
to be driven out by insensitive authority rather than lured
out by a pretty blonde.

The present crisis in the priesthood then is not whether
they should be allowed to be married or whether even
married men or indeed women should be called to the
ministry. The clerical issue is a complete, honest, professional re-education of the priestly function in a world
which is skeptical of magic. It views the priest as an insurance-policy agent and a faceless functionary at baptisms,
marriages, and funerals. The heart of the matter is to give
a new dynamism to the priest, whether he be married or
celibate—full time or part time.

On July 29, 1968, Pope Paul VI ended five years of uncertainty over how he viewed modern methods of birth
control with the official presentation of a papal encyclical
letter that upheld the prohibition of all artificial means of
contraception. The letter, called "Of Human Life," reaffirmed that Roman Catholics might limit the size of their
families only by the rhythm method, confining the marriage
act to a woman's infertile period. The main message of
Pope Paul's declaration was his reaffirmation of the teaching

proclaimed forty years ago by Pope Pius XI—"That each and every marriage act must remain open to the transmission of life."

The document set in motion a critical situation in the Church, a crisis of conscience for numerous Catholics who during Pope Paul's five years' silence accepted it as a matter of personal decision. Reactions to the news were swift and polarized. Sheen, at the time Bishop of Rochester, likened birth control today to violence. He described Pope Paul as a man who dared to oppose that world and said he would be crucified for his position. Sheen said that violence is a dominant idea in the modern world. Violence is the laying of hands on life, either to maim it, to destroy it, or to annul it.

In a talk in Dublin, Ireland, in July of 1969, Sheen condemned the mini-popes who dared to oppose Paul on this question. To applause from his Irish audience, Sheen ended his homily in a typically dramatic manner. Referring to those who had a view contrary to the Pope's, he said: "I would rather be wrong with him [Pope Paul] than right with them." Sheen always referred to birth control as birth patrol, for those who practice it, according to him, believe neither in birth nor control. In April 1971, in a landmark decision, the Vatican ruled that the priests who disputed the conservative Cardinal O'Boyle's (of Washington, D.C.) ruling on birth control must follow his and the Pope's teaching, saying, "Conscience is not a law unto itself."

Needless to say, Pope Paul got a lot of backing from

bishops throughout the world. On the other hand, some, such as the Belgian, Dutch, and Canadian bishops, were more cautious and deliberate, praising the document as an ideal but emphasizing the primacy of conscience.

The noted Swiss theologian, Hans Kung, author of a controversial work on papal infallibility, one of the great architects of Vatican II, said that Pope Paul's ban on contraception demonstrated not only that the Pope was not infallible but also that he was wrong. Kung continued that there was reason to fear that the Pauline Encyclical would open a new "Galileo Case"—a reference to the seventeenth-century astronomer who was condemned by the Church for having "heretically proclaimed that the earth moved around the sun." One of the most blistering attacks on the encyclical came from the normally mild-mannered, world-renowned theologian, German-born Father Bernard Haring. He called for a rescue operation of the Pope from the stifling inbred Curia. Haring was on the Pope's commission of two hundred who studied the question of birth control. He reported that 80 percent of the commission were in favor of liberalizing the Church's birth-control laws. The question again has polarized the Church, and there the sizzling situation stands. Here again we see Sheen is party line in things theological, but progessive in matters social. His policy would be that of Pope Paul's "not to diminish the number of guests, rather to multiply the bread that is to be shared." Of course, Sheen is totally opposed to abortion.

CHAPTER

11

SHEEN AND THE POPES AND
PRINCES OF THE CHURCH

THE WORLD in which Sheen met his calvary is defined by the personalities who have dominated it.

Of all the great figures of our time, one of the most revered was Eugenio Pacelli, known universally as Pope Pius XII. He led the Church through one of the most turbulent eras in the history of mankind, including the rise of nazism, of fascism, World War II, the postwar menace of communism, the Korean War, the unrest in the Soviet satellites, and the Middle East crises. In 1939, in a Europe threatened by war, the great antagonist of communism, the courageous Pope Pius XI, died. Pope Pius XI had advised Sheen to speak out against the red menace which he saw threatened all Europe. In one of the shortest conclaves in history, Eugenio Pacelli—Pius XI's astute Secretary of State —was elected to succeed him.

Pacelli was born in Rome of patrician patronage. He was

in poor health as a boy and as did Montini (Pope Paul VI) later on for the same reason, he pursued all his studies outside the seminary. He was a very intelligent student, languages being his forte. In 1899 he was ordained a priest. He began work in the Vatican Foreign Office, after a few years of postgraduate studies. His friend and mentor was the prestigious Cardinal Gasparri. Pacelli served under four popes: Leo XIII, Pius X, Benedict XV and Pius XI. When he worked in the Secretariat of State, he became friends with a likable American, Francis Spellman, who also worked there, but in a much minor position. Thus began the Pacelli-Spellman axis. Pacelli's only overseas stint was the time he spent in Munich as the Pope's representative to Germany. There he saw the rise of nazism. In Munich he could do very little for peace. When Pacelli was made a cardinal, his titular Church in Rome was Saints John and Paul, the same Church he gave as titular when, later on as Pope, he presented Spellman with the Red Hat. Pius, however, was a prisoner of the Vatican. Very few could ever see him privately in the evening; among those who could were the late Father Bea, S.J., his personal confessor and later Cardinal Bea, the great ecumenist and one of the architects of Vatican Council II. Count Enrico Galeazzi, Governor of the Vatican State, could also visit him alone, as could the Count's half brother, Professor Ricardo Galeazzi, Pius' physician, who showed great disloyalty and poor taste by hawking still and movie pictures of the Pontiff's last moments. In addition to these visits, the man from New York,

Francis Spellman, could come in the back door when he was in the Eternal City.

Pius, as we see, was very close to Cardinal Spellman. However, Sheen had a private audience each year for half an hour with the Pope, who recognized Sheen's great ability. It is a pity that he did not utilize Sheen more by giving him a more powerful position in the Church. Lesser men than he have received positions more responsible. Spellman must certainly have prevailed on Pius not to promote his stubborn, but extremely gifted, underling. Pius, like all men, grew old, and not gracefully. He became more and more aloof, and very few could get to see him. The fact that his brilliant assistant, Montini, broke through the papal coterie during one of Pius' illnesses apparently ended in his being exiled to Milan. But God's ways are not man's ways, and paradoxically he would come back as number one to the Vatican. However, the reverse was true in the case of Sheen —he never succeeded Spellman as Archbishop of New York.

It is now a matter of history that the late Pope Pius XII, who was in power during Europe's long dark night of Nazi hell, worked incessantly behind the scenes to mitigate suffering, but surprisingly enough he never raised his prestigious voice to condemn openly and unequivocally the horrendous crimes of the Nazis. The fact that he never raised his voice is not challenged today. There is a debate about the question whether his reticence was justified. Many claim he did everything he could within reason. The present Pope attests to this belief by setting in motion formal proceedings for Pope Pius XII's canonization. His detractors, such as playwright Rolf Hochult, who wrote the play *The Deputy*, portrayed him as one whose silence pointed to cowardice, complicity, and cynicism, a sinner and no saint. The truth may be more the following: Pope Paul VI, in an article in the English Roman Catholic journal *The Tablet*, contended an outright condemnation of the Nazis by the Pope would have been of no avail and most likely harmful. Apparently Pope Pius told a wartime pilgrim, "Tell everyone . . . that the Pope is in anguish and with them (but) after many tears and many prayers, came to the conclusion that a protest from me would not only not help anyone, but would arouse the most ferocious anger against the Jews and multiply acts of cruelty because they are undefended." Hochult's allegations that Pope Pius XII was a coward and not a profile in courage is simply not true. Pius showed moral and physical courage on numerous occasions and his personal holiness was never called into question. Pope Pius' hesitance to oppose nazism openly, and Sheen's failure to have an eyeball-to-eyeball confrontation with Spellman probably prevented each from being a giant in his time.

Pius' failing, if failing it was, was his utter reliance on diplomacy. He could have condemned Nazi atrocities and have offered to release German Catholics from obeying their government. This might have marshaled some conscientious Germans against the cruelties committed in the name of Germany. Maybe Pius could have taken the suggestion of a Protestant leader who advocated that Pius

assume leadership of an ecumenical religious movement unit-
ing all Christians against aggressive wars. Pius for one reason
or another never took up the challenge.

Pius XII was a very gifted man. His encyclicals, his addresses, and his understanding of modern-day science will
give him a great place in Church history. Seemingly, however, he was a one-man show; he could not delegate authority. How place him in secular history? Much time must
pass before this man can be truly weighed in the scales of
history. Contemporary opinions are choked by emotions
and prejudices. History, however, will recount one thing:
Pius XII was a saintly man, and death, which comes to
beggars and kings, to popes as well as priests, came to Pius
XII. All peoples were shaken at his death. The Angelo
Guiseppe Roncalli, who was waiting in the wings, was
elected his successor, and took the world by storm. The
miracle of the twentieth century had just begun.

The big question was: Should the Church show the way
to the secular world, clinging to the City of God in fear of
contamination from the City of Man? The learned Pius said
No, but he never got around to do anything about it. It was
left to John XXIII, neither an intellectual nor a theologian,
to expose Catholicism to the forces of change. John's calling of Vatican Council II was an historic event to update
the Church—the aggiornamento, which he called it.

John was a very astute man, full of charity. He wanted
all men to be his friends. He gave many priests audiences.
To Sheen at one such audience he remarked that he knew

all about the Sheen-Spellman donnybrook. Spellman lost some of his power at Pius' death, yet John must have felt Spellman was right, otherwise he would have promoted Sheen.

One night in a Roman hotel room during one of the sessions of Vatican Council II, Sheen got a call that Pope John wanted to see him. Sheen's first reaction was that it was a bogus message—the Pope would hardly see him without an appointment, and certainly not at night. Sheen, to be sure however, went to the Vatican. He was ushered in immediately to the papal apartments. Pope John took him for a tour of his own private quarters, which was a rare privilege. On leaving, John asked Sheen to visit his own native town of Soto-il-monte in Bergamo.

John changed the history of Church relations—far more than the shrewd, blunt Pius XI or the ascetic, aristocratic Pius XII. John seemed like a universal Father. His encyclical *Mater et Magistra*, on social issues, and *Pacem en Terris*, on peace, will go down in history. He had a tremendous sense of the human. On being asked how many worked in the Vatican, he retorted, "Only half of them." He began a soft line on communism. He believed in dialogue with his adversaries. Not all Catholics were in agreement with all Pope John's policies. His "opening to the left" some claimed caused a tremendous vote for communism in Italy. Right-wing Italian Catholics called John the Red Pope when he received in audience *Tzuestias'* former editor, Adzhubel, who was Khrushchev's son-in-law. Many die-

hard conservatives were probably aghast at some of his
positions, but few had anything but genuine love for John
as a person. He was an unaffected, human, humble priest
who revered people rather than ideas. John planted a seed.
He knew someone else would reap the harvest.

Many people have spent much time in probing the secret
of Pope John's diplomatic success. It was not an intellectual
process. It was the nature of the man. People always trusted
him because they all wished him well. In human relations,
he was guided by his heart, and most of the time he was
right. Pope John knew how to reach and win the hearts
of his fellow men. He did not preach to them; he understood them. One of Sheen's problems all his life was the
fact that he was not close to the common man. He became
a Hollywood type who lived in a dream world of myth.
Morris West, the great Australian writer, has observed:
"If you lose contact with the common man, you can lose
the faith." That was John's secret. He attained the highest
dignities in the Church—Bishop, Papal Nuncio in France,
Cardinal of Venice, and Vicar of Christ—yet he was always
himself. As Nuncio in Paris, at a diplomatic reception, he
was sitting near a lady with a rather low-cut dress. When
fresh figs were passed around John quipped, "A fig for me;
a fig leaf for you, madame." Another time in Paris, a car-
penter came to his residence to do some repairs. Apparently
he hit his thumb with the hammer and began to utter all
types of oaths and imprecations. The Papal Nuncio stuck
his head out of his office door and said, "Shame. Why don't

you say 'Merde' like the rest of us." When we were really enjoying Pope John and taking him for granted, cancer cut him down. It was said we could not stand another John. Oh, yes, we could. John XXIII, probably the finest pope in Christendom's history, was dead. A conclave was in session to elect a successor. I helped Sheen with a telecast which he gave on the election of a pope, in which Sheen announced he had a name in mind. He did not mention it, but it was Montini who had entered the conclave a pope and defied tradition by coming out a pope. He had been the odds-on favorite of journalists, clerics, and the betting population of Rome's cafés. The man who left Rome with one suitcase and thirty cases of books, in apparent disgrace, had come back a commander-in-chief. He had a good blend of ecclesiastical experience behind him: eight years in charge of Milan, Italy's largest diocese, following three decades of efficient, unobtrusive service in the Vatican Secretariat of State. He was facing a difficult role. He was like a Lyndon Johnson following a charismatic John Kennedy, and somehow, like the man from Texas, he would never capture the people's hearts.

What happened in the Roman conclave is officially a secret. But a secret in Rome seems to be like a public announcement anywhere else. Apparently some progressives voted for the outstanding Belgian Cardinal, Leon-Josef Suenens, to remind the conclave that the Bishop of Rome need not necessarily be Italian. Maybe the time has come for a non-Italian Pope. Paul VI is a complex man—a lonely, melancholy individual. While he was in Milan, he visited her Communist districts. He became known as the worker's archbishop. On his visits to office buildings, mines, and factories, he carried a portable mass kit in a briefcase. He looked like a Milanese businessman. He was secretly dubbed, "Jesus Christ's Chairman of the Board." He conducted Billy Graham-like crusades in the Milan streets. The Church in the United States could have used Sheen in such crusades, with his power to sway crowds.

When Montini worked in the Vatican for Pius XII, he wanted to break that closed club called the Curia. As Pope he is moving to internationalize the governing body of the Church. Paul is more cautious than John in promoting the Church and in fostering concord with the Communists. A protégé of Pius XII, a close friend of John XXIII, he has emerged with an image all his own. John was an intuitive, charismatic prophet who threw open the windows and doors of the Church to let in fresh air without worrying about or even fully understanding the consequences. Paul, on the other hand, is a precise, detailed technician. He has kept the door open, but is continually checking the thermostat.

The Curia has left its mark on Paul. He is an indecisive intellectual, dubbed Hamlet by Pope John himself. Paul is fearful of a split in an already polarized Church. During John's reign of four years, four hundred years of history were changed. Everybody is spinning, and it is going to take years before, if ever, things settle down again. Some see in Paul a real pope of Transition. His wish is not to shake up anything, not to break the Church in two, not to allow the formation against one another of a triumphant majority and a crushed minority. Some writers, such as John Cogley, believe, however, that Paul is presiding over the dissolution of the Holy Roman Empire.

Paul has become the Jet Pope. He was the first pope since Peter to set foot on the Holy Land. Someone quipped he went there to pay the bill for the Last Supper. Another said: He went there to start the Church all over again. His meeting with Patriarch Athenagoras of the Eastern Orthodox Church was certainly meaningful. Shalom was his greeting.

Paul's next trip was to the Eucharistic Congress in India. He was received by millions. At a press conference in Bombay he called on the world to close the armaments race and devote its resources and energies instead to fraternal assistance for developing countries. It was strange that Sheen was not invited as a guest, as he has been instrumental in sending millions of dollars to alleviate hunger in India.

Pope Paul's trip on October 5, 1965, to the United Nations was really historic. Every moment of the trip was covered by TV. CBS had Sheen as a guest commentator to help out Harry Reasoner. Pope Paul's warm personality came across very well on his trip to the United States. His helping hand to the shuffling Spellman was moving. Some found Sheen's description of Pope Paul's visit rather too dramatic. Reasoner, the veteran CBS reporter, asked Sheen the difference between Paul and John, to which he responded, "John broke the ice, and Paul is enjoying the swim." Paul's speech at the United Nations was dramatic, especially when he said, "War—war—never again." The pontifical mass at Yankee Stadium was impressive and colorful. Some called it the Stadium of Maris, Mantle, Montini, and DiMaggio.

On May 13, 1967, Pope Paul VI visited Fatima. It was the fiftieth anniversary of the apparition of Our Lady of Fatima to the three children. The reason for the trip was, in his own words, to seek Mary's intercession in favor of unity in the Church and peace in the world. The Pope celebrated Mass before a million people and in his talk called for harmony in the Church and peace in the world. The Pope greeted the only survivor among the three children, who reported seeing the Fatima vision, Lucia dos Santos, now a Carmelite nun in her sixties. He also conferred with the controversial Portuguese dictator, Antonio Salazar.

In November and December of 1970, Pope Paul, who has described himself as an "apostle on the move," made seven stopovers on his Asian tour: Manila, Sydney, Iran, the Samoan Islands, Indonesia, Hong Kong, and Ceylon. The Missionary Pope used the visit to preach the gospel of peace in Asia and to visit the Islands of the Pacific as a demonstration of the Church's interest in all men everywhere. Never in history has a pope traveled so far. Pope Paul has visited the five continents. The Jet Pope likes to be known as "a fisher of men." Paul was lucky to leave the predominantly Catholic Philippine Islands alive, where he was the object of an alleged assassination attempt at Manila Airport by a knife-wielding Bolivian painter.

To encourage ecumenism with Protestants, the Second Vatican Council did not emphasize devotion to Mary. Some observers saw in Paul's trip to Fatima the intention of curbing any extremes in the de-emphasis of Mary. Sheen was a guest commentator on ABC's satellite coverage of the Pope's visit to Fatima. This time he was excellent. Paul made other trips, to Greece and Turkey to Uganda and Switzerland. He went to the most critical area in the Church, Latin America, by visiting Bogota in Colombia. He visited the Far East, Japan, Australia, and the Philippines. The Pope seems to think, as President Eisenhower did in the last years of his presidency, that personal diplomacy could heal world problems, which it did not. The issues that divide Pope Paul's Church are deeper than personal pilgrimages can heal. Pope Paul seems to be pained at the present crisis in the Church. Not long ago, he told Archbishop Sheen in an audience that he begins each day by reading correspondence from all over the world. "There is a thorn in almost every letter," Paul said. "When I put my head against the pillow at night, it rests upon a crown of thorns."

I suppose that is the difference between John and Paul. John was optimistic by nature; Paul is pessimistic. John would see the roses among the thorns; Paul sees the thorns among the roses. Pope Paul knew all the details about the row between Sheen and Spellman. Yet he, too, never gave

Sheen a prestigious position in the Church. Sheen resigned in Rochester—in a diocese divided. Will Pope Paul at seventy-five step down in a Church divided?

Luigi Barzini, the Italian writer, crystalizes the true role of the Church, which is to connect man with the Infinite, hence the Catholic dilemma: "If the Church modernizes too far it will lose the past and immortality. If the Church does not modernize enough it will lose the people." It was in January of 1959, when his pontificate was in its infancy, that Pope John had a conversation with his gruff but kind-hearted Cardinal Secretary of State Domenico Tardini. They discussed the condition of the world and how the Church could meet its challenges. Suddenly, the words "A council" sprung from John's lips. "Si, Si, un concilio," replied Tardini. A new dawn was breaking for all Christendom.

Pope John had to work strenuously at changing the atmosphere of quasi-adoration that surrounded his predecessor, Pope Pius XII. Pius ran a one-man show, and John had to restore the ecclesiastical organism. Pope John in calling a council proclaimed for Christendom a New Pentecost, a Revolution of Love. The paradox of the "Fat Christ," however, was that in his loving efforts to renew the Church, he conferred a cleansing anguish upon its inner life that leaves its members today bitterly polarized and divided.

Sheen did not speak at the first three sessions of the council. There was a lot of talk of good guys and bad guys at it; it was almost like a John Wayne cowboy movie. In a witty speech to newsmen in Rome during the first session, Sheen satirized this split between liberals and conservatives. He described how the First Council of Jerusalem in 52 A.D. might have been reported by a modern journalist. He had the Carthage daily paper headline a complaint about the original lag in starting the work of the Church, there being a delay between the ascension and the descent of the Holy Spirit upon the apostles.

Sheen, once speaking about polarization, said that the liberals and conservatives are in tension and opposition, but that the Divine Craftsman would unite them. Catholicism in the United States has had the touch of Madison Avenue about it; it has been called Chancery Catholicism. Real power in the United States Church up to now had been with the clerical politicians and administrators rather than with theologians and intellectuals. Vatican Council II has described the Church as the People of God. It will be a long time, however, before the real power is with the people. One of the best advocates of shared responsibility in the Church among pope, bishops, priests, and people is the Cardinal of the new wave, Leon-Josef Suenens of Belgium. He wants a loyal opposition in the Church. He is an advocate of reform within the structure. His battle is against juridicism, but not against justice; against authoritarianism, but not against authority; against legalism, but not against the law; against rigidity, but not against order; against uniformity, but not against unity.

The Church in America has been dubbed by Sheen "The Via Dollar-osa." There has been an ecclesiastical bureaucracy in the United States Church which tends toward uniformity. Sheen once thundered to a stunned congregation of clerics: "For the love of Christ, stop being administrators and start being shepherds of souls." It will take another generation or two to produce the new bishop who will be a shepherd rather than an administrator. Many people, and some priests, however, are impatient and are unwilling to play that waiting game.

To whom does the Church in the United States look to lead it into the third millennium? Academically to men like Father Ted Hesburgh. He is president of Notre Dame, which was once the Catholic West Point, but is now in the mainstream of American life. Notre Dame, which was once famous only for its Fighting Irish football team, is through Hesburgh's efforts one of the leading Catholic institutions of higher learning in the world.

Or will the Church look to the intellectuals such as the Austrian-born priest, the Christian rebel, Ivan Illich, who is a folk hero to the Catholic Left. Illich is a thorn in the side of the Vatican, a friend of Latin American rebels and avant-garde European bishops, priests, and nuns. His philosophy is a kind of radical humanism pitted against middle-class complacency.

Or will the future of the Church be with the people, who are, according to Vatican Council II, The Church? Probably some leaders will emerge from the people who will be influenced by a philosophy of hope and urged on by a philosophy of risk. Then the New Day that dawned in 1959 when Pope John called the Vatican Council II will shine in all its splendor, and we would need a Sheen to herald it in.

Another controversial figure in Sheen's lifetime was Cardinal McIntyre, who for many years cast a long shadow over the West Coast, but it was owing more to his financial than to his intellectual stature. There are about 1.5 million Catholics in Los Angeles. In his day McIntyre used to build six new churches and fifteen schools every year. McIntyre was a late vocation. He had a newspaper route to put him through night school. He worked for a time on Wall Street. He was a protégé of the bishop-maker, Spellman. McIntyre was succeeded by Irish-born Timothy Manning, a thin, taut intellectual who had been called "The Sheen of the West" because of his oratory. Sheen in his day would have been an ideal choice for Los Angeles. The Microphone of God would have fitted in with the Beverly Hills clan.

John Cardinal Wright is a tall man with a stately paunch and a Dorchester accent. He is what is known in Boston as a Southie. He is the highest ranking American in the Vatican, where he heads the Congregation for the clergy. He learns about his job by staying away from his desk. The ubiquitous prelate turns up all over the world lecturing priests, hopefully listening to them. His rise in the Church has been meteoric. He was secretary to Cardinal O'Connell of Boston, who was nicknamed "Gangplank Bill" because of his frequent junkets. Wright was secretary and auxiliary bishop to Richard Cardinal Cushing, first Bishop of Worcester, Massachusetts, and for ten years Bishop of Pittsburgh until he was summoned to Rome to become a member of the elite Vatican Club, the Roman Curia. Wright was once known as the intellectual of the American Church. He is a liberal in social issues, but conservative in theological matters. He is an able man, but some consider Lefty Wright (as he was affectionately known in Pittsburgh), the ebullient heavyweight of the American Church, to be more right than left. Some think him a theological lightweight in modern Church movements who enjoys playing Church and all the falderal that goes with being a Prince of that Church.

Wright, unlike Sheen, played his clerical cards well and thus gained advancement in the ecclesiastical big league. He delivered a dramatic and moving eulogy at the funeral services of Richard Cardinal Cushing, the earthy, blunt, craggy-jawed son of an Irish blacksmith, the man with the gravelly voice and the golden heart—Boston's Pope John and a twentieth-century St. Francis of Assisi. Wright said, "We commend this valiant newsmaker to history—this holy man—zealous priest—uncommon prelate to God." The Cardinal, (The Cahdnal) as he was affectionately referred to in Boston, was laid to rest in a crypt at St. Coletta's School some twenty miles south of the Hub City. The school is for retarded children, or exceptional children as Cushing preferred to call them. It was a favorite charity.

Cardinal Cushing in his inimitable South Boston accent used to tell the following story on himself: that he died and went to the golden gates to be judged. St. Peter welcomed him, but to his dismay he could not find the Cardinal's name on the list. So, brokenhearted, he sent him down below. He quickly, however, discovered his mistake. Cushing's name was listed under "The Irish" rather than under "The Cardinals." Peter swiftly sent an angel to fetch him. The angel was met by a fallen one at the door. "Oh, no you don't. Cardinal Cushing promised us one million dollars to install a cooling system."

A child in a Boston first-grade Catholic School swallowed a quarter and it stuck in his throat. One of the sisters quipped: "Send for the Cardinal, he will get it out of him."

These stories underscore the Cardinal's great sense of humor, his unbelievable dedication to the underprivileged and cast-offs of society. Who was this blunt, unpredictable prelate who was more the prince of the people than of his Church?

Sheen has written of the lately mourned Cardinal Archbishop of Boston: "Cardinal Cushing was only tethered in Boston. His pasturage was as wide as the priesthood. From a physical and medical point of view, Cushing had no right to be alive. He lived because God willed him to have an indomitable spirit in a suffering body. His influence, his radiating charity, his power to communicate wisdom and to invoke love from sheep and lambs came not from a healthy mind in a sound body, but from a spiritual mind in a broken body. It is easy to give up money, it is hard to give up the hours and minutes in which one is exhausted. Each priest has seen in Cushing the new vow of poverty of the twentieth century: the impoverishment of time, energy, and repose for the glory of the Church. They know well that Cushing like a great ship moved wearily in shallow waters of human praise. Thus he who never sought to be nationally known was nationally loved; greater still, he who never sought to be internationally known is the most loved of all in the flung missions of the Church, in Africa, Asia, Oceania, and Latin America. Someone has described Cushing as a massive muscular man with deep-etched lines in his face. Hearing him I thought of Al Smith—and looking at him—Abraham Lincoln. Then as the impact of his words gripped me, I thought of Albert Schweitzer—Smith—Lincoln and put them together and you had Cardinal Cushing."

Some years ago, when Cushing was extremely ill and on the verge of retiring, he wrote to Sheen saying he wanted him to succeed him as Archbishop of Boston. Man at times proposes, but Rome disposes. There was much in common in the work of both men, and yet their personalities were completely different. Cushing was always one of the common folk, an unpretentious prelate from South Boston. Sheen is a press agent's dream of a mystic. Both were intensely committed to alleviating the lot of the poor at home and overseas. Both were great fund-raisers. Sheen is a brilliant orator. Cushing, while the content of his remarks was excellent, had the rasping voice of a fish peddler. The length of his talks was notorious; so much so that someone once quipped to him, "Your Eminence—you don't have to be eternal to be immortal."

Cushing encouraged all his clergy to stay in touch with the times. There was a lot of *The Last Hurrah* about him. There was also a generous measure of the spirit of Vatican Council II in him. He was Boston's answer to "Good Pope John," as he dubbed him. Cushing by his activities epitomizes the stirring of that awakening giant—the Roman Catholic Church in the United States. The Church in America has ceased to be an immigrant Church; it has come of age. It has, however, to have a more intellectual background—the gospels, not the *Wall Street Journal*, must be its Bible. The emphasis must be on building cathedrals of the spirit; the era of brick and mortar is over. Sheen and Cushing in their distinct ways were giants of the American Church. Sheen is a man who presented an intellectual image of the Church to middle America. By his urbanity, wit, and wisdom he created an atmosphere where the Church was accepted in the secular city. On the other hand, Cushing was a kind of Christ in concrete. He spoke the language of the common man and was at ease with him. Toward the end of his life, when it was rumored that he was going to resign, he was told that Cardinal Wright had his eye on the seat of Boston. Cushing's remark was typical: "He might have his eye on it, but I've got my ass on it."

Cushing was a tireless worker, he was a doer rather than a thinker. His true greatness was his extraordinary love of people and the good will he fostered with people of all faiths. Way before it was fashionable, he was preaching in Protestant churches and Jewish synagogues. He was an unorthodox man. He once entertained a delegation of visiting New York policemen by rushing into a pub with his mitre on and ordering drinks all around. When he visited the schools in his cardinal's robes, he used to tell the children he was Santa Claus. For a long time he and the other man from Boston, Spellman, apparently were cool to each other. Rumor had it that Spellman prevailed upon his friend Pope Pius XII not to give a Red Hat to Cushing. It was left up to Pope John in 1958 to honor Cushing and Boston.

Cushing did not stay long at the Vatican Council sessions, remaining about three weeks each time. To applause in the assembly, however, he gave two stirring talks on religious liberty and on the declaration that the Jews were not guilty of the death of Christ. He captured the spirit of Pope John, about whom Cushing said: "He was the only man who ever understood me, and I don't even understand myself." Maybe some day it will be revealed how Cushing became a cardinal and Archbishop of Little Vatican, Boston—and how Sheen, who seemed to be destined for higher things, ended up as Bishop of Rochester.

Cushing made no bones about backing John F. Kennedy's quest for the White House and he became nationally known when he delighted the President and the TV audience at the inauguration of 1961 by steadfastly continuing his long invocation after smoke began to form from the lectern

in front of him. Referring to the invocation, Kennedy said,
"I don't think he [Cushing] went on too long. It was the
first inauguration of a Catholic President in the history of
the United States, and Cardinal Spellman had to watch it
on television." Spellman had backed Richard Nixon in the
1960 election and Kennedy did not invite him to the ceremonies. Cushing had to assume a more somber role in November 1963 when he conducted the funeral service in St.
Matthews in Washington for the slain President. He was
comforting the Kennedys soon again at the brutal assassination of Robert. He consoled Rose during Joseph, Sr.'s, long
illness and subsequent death. He got into hot water when he
staunchly defended Jacqueline Kennedy when she married
Greek shipping magnate Aristotle Onassis in October of
1968. Cushing admitted that she had conferred with him
before the marriage and that he had rejected requests to
try to stop the union.

"This idea of saying she's excommunicated, she's a public
sinner—what a lot of nonsense," he then said. "Only God
knows who is a sinner, who is not." Later on he called her
"a wonderful girl," and also remarked, "I assure you she is
a valiant woman of modern times. Someone had to step up
and say a kind word in her support . . . I stepped forward
to say something that nobody else would say, and I was
inundated from all over the country and all parts of the
world." Cushing was shocked and personally very hurt over
all the abuse hurled at him because of his stance—some of it
couched in the language of the gutter. He said he was going

to resign. The Vatican refused to accept his offer. Jacqueline Onassis said at the Cardinal's death: "I loved him and will miss him terribly for the rest of my life. Cardinal Cushing's suffering has ended and the world has lost one of the greatest men who ever lived. His life was built on love; to heal rather than to divide."

One of the Cardinal's great enthusiasms was Latin America, where he dispatched hundreds of missionaries and millions of dollars, years before it was fashionable to champion the Third World. Cushing was helping everywhere there was need. He collected almost $3 million for ransom of Cubans after the Bay of Pigs invasion. Unfortunately, however, the years began to take their toll and the strain began to show in his craggy, furrowed face. He was suffering from asthma, emphysema, ulcers, and cancer. On his seventy-fifth birthday, on September 8, 1970, Cushing stepped down. Surprisingly, he was replaced by a little-known Bishop Humberto Medeiros of the Brownsville diocese in Texas. Medeiros was born in the Azores. For the first time in 124 years Boston had a non-Irish prelate at the Hub's helm. It was twilight for the Irish. A new era in American Church history had begun. The choice of a Portuguese for archbishop of the Irish-dominated archdiocese of Boston has shown the Church in America has reached a healthy adulthood. It was something more than a mere changing of the guard. Cushing, despite his progressive programs, represented really the Church of the pre-Vatican II while Medeiros is symbolic of "the new bishop" dedicated to social activism that is attempting to lead the Church in an age of unrest and turmoil. The dying Cushing was privileged to see his successor take over his place in Boston. In a moving and poignant farewell address at Medeiros' installation, the great Cushing got a standing ovation.

Less than a month later he was dead. Edward Kennedy said at the Cardinal's death: "Cardinal Cushing had so much strength—so much tolerance—so much compassion—so much dignity that one wonders if we of a different generation will be able to fill the void. For we will never see the like of him again."

As were many of his distinguished predecessors and contemporaries in the Church described above, Sheen was a friend and advisor of Popes. Yet, instead of a Roman promotion, he found his calvary in Rochester.

CHAPTER
12

CALVARY IN ROCHESTER

TALKING ABOUT Easter, Sheen said, "The law He gave us was clear: life is a struggle. Unless there is a cross in our lives, there will never be the empty tomb—unless there is a crown of thorns, there will never be the halo of light—unless there is a Good Friday, there will never be an Easter Sunday."

Some thought that Rochester would have been Sheen's Easter Sunday, but unfortunately it turned out to be his Good Friday. On October 26, 1966, then in his early seventies, Fulton J. Sheen, known to millions throughout the world, was appointed by Pope Paul to succeed the aging Kearney as Bishop of Rochester. In his typically dramatic manner he accepted the appointment as an opportunity to be closer to souls, commenting, "I'll be just a bit closer to the people than I was before. I'm a soldier, and the general has told me to go to Rochester, and I'm very happy. I love

people; I love souls. In fact, souls are the only reality in
the world."

Few saw Sheen's appointment as a promotion. Was he
being kicked upstairs, apparently to make an easy transition
for Spellman's heir apparent, Terence Cooke? When Sheen
was appointed to Rochester, someone wrote to him saying,
"What kind of Church do you work for? It sends a thousand horse power tractor to plough an acre of land."

On the evening of December 15, 1966, thousands of
Catholics and non-Catholics crowded downtown Rochester
to see its new Catholic Bishop, a TV star in his own right.
He remarked: "Rochester—I have no further plans." Rumor
had it he might be staying in Rochester for only a short
time, that he would be moving on to a higher post, such
as Los Angeles. Early in the day Sheen was installed at the
Sacred Heart Cathedral. He said at his installation: "A new
bishop in a diocese is something like a new baby in a family.
There is no doubt about the child being loved. The problem is: 'What kind of a child will he be?' "

At the luncheon honoring Sheen on the day of his installation, Spellman was the first to speak. He said he had
mixed feelings of sorrow and joy at Bishop Sheen's position.
"You belong not only to the ages, but to the world."
Bishop Kearney, the retiring Bishop of Rochester, said of
him: "It is preposterous for anyone to attempt to introduce
Bishop Fulton Sheen to an audience. There are only three
kinds of people in all the world who don't know who he is.
They include those who cannot read, those who have never

listened to the radio, and those who have never looked at a TV set."

"The problem is: 'What kind of a child will he be?'" Would the renowned TV star, author, and orator make the difficult transition into the people's bishop in the spirit of Vatican Council II? William Buckley has described Sheen as an enigma. He was dubbed Agent 007 in Rochester, and he almost managed to have a headline a day, although his relationship with the press was far from a happy one. On arrival in Rochester he did not run according to the pundits. He seemed to be espousing liberal cause after liberal cause, to the dismay of the conservative city. He had very little parish experience, none except, forty years previously, in the two St. Patrick's, miles apart: St. Patrick's, London, England; and St. Patrick's, Peoria, Illinois. God's press agent arrived in Rochester with the image of a conservative, photogenic, articulate bishop. Millions of people of all faiths and of none would remember him as best-selling author, a charismatic TV performer, and Mr. Church in the United States in the 1950's. He was better known as an interpreter of his faith, a company man, not an innovator. Rochester was pleased it was getting a worldwide celebrity who was no boat rocker. That was what they expected, but they were in for a surprise.

Sheen is a fascinating man who, infatuated by his own ego, could not really respond to friendship. At the core, the normal sympathies that ordinary men and women enjoy were not in him. He lacked the courage to be really great.

Sheen is a consummate egocentric, a skillful actor who mesmerizes audiences, who flows with the mood of the crowd—and this is not intellectually honest. He is a kind of Everett Dirksen, playing all sides of all issues to suit the mood of the time and his own needs. I remember walking down Fifth Avenue in New York one day on our way to lunch. Two old ladies stopped him. One of them asked him for his autograph. As he gladly signed it, the other lady looked at me and said, "Isn't he a great actor?" In Rochester he was to play his toughest role in his long theatrical career, before his toughest audience. Would he get a clerical Academy Award?

Sheen had reached a pinnacle that few humans do: he is a living legend. Rochester is the epitome of middle-class America and it was star struck at Sheen's arrival. The city that took him to its heart soon would be bitterly torn over him. One priest said of Sheen's policies, "We have only to stall him off for four years until he reaches retirement age. Then the whole nonsense will be quickly forgotten and we'll get back to the tried and trusted methods that always served us well." When Sheen resigned, one Rochesterian remarked: "Rochester is back in the American League again."

Within a week of his arrival, Sheen plunged into the middle of a sizzling civil rights dispute. His immediate involvement was in a battle between Fight (Freedom—Integration—God—Honor—Today), a militant civil rights movement, and Eastman Kodak. He took on the establishment.

As a result he was never really accepted, and consequently his thousand days in Rochester would not be happy. The basis of the struggle with Eastman Kodak was that Fight charged Kodak refused to honor an agreement with Fight, apparently made by one of their executives, that Kodak would hire and train a stipulated number of unemployed blacks. When the company did not act accordingly, Fight claimed they had been double-crossed. A bitter dispute occurred which got national publicity. Sheen did not launch a frontal attack against Eastman Kodak. However, he showed in no uncertain terms where his sympathies lay. He had a first again. He picked as a "Vicar for the urban poor," a young priest who was the only white member of Fight. While the struggle was going on, Sheen addressed a packed Chamber of Commerce banquet. His theme was the city's racial problem. He compared Rochester to a beautiful woman with a pimple on her nose—the racial discrimination. Shortly afterward the chairman of Eastman Kodak, leaving after the Sunday service, replying to the minister's solicitous inquiry after his health, quipped, "I'm fine, thanks, except for this blemish on my nose." A lot of people thought Sheen acted too hastily in an issue he knew too little about. Some believed Fight to be too militant. Was Sheen again using the occasion for his extraordinary need for publicity and attention, or was he really committed to the alleviation of the plight of the urban poor?

He also became involved immediately in the ecumenical movement. He interchanged pulpits with ministers and

rabbis, so much so that someone observed, "Catholics tell
me if they want to see their new bishop, they have to go to
Jewish services." On an Ash Wednesday, Sheen, with his
usual flair for the dramatic, and at times the sensational, announced he was giving parish property valued at $680,000
to the federal government for low-income housing. The
property consisted of church, convent, rectory, and school.
Sheen said, "The parish was offered not because the property was not needed, but rather in order that through a
sacrificial gift, the diocese might alleviate the plight of the
poor." This was an excellent idea, but it was handled badly
by Sheen. The Church should put itself on the line and give
an example of leadership by divesting itself of some of its
property to alleviate poverty and eliminate slum conditions
which corrode the human spirit. The Church has no right
to build million-dollar complexes used once a week, while
millions live in slums which destroy human dignity and
decency. The paradox of the institutional Church today is
the penniless Christ crucified on a cross of gold. Sheen,
however, by his grandstand play, and his tendency to capture immediate attention, did not foresee the implications
involved. In this age of coresponsibility, he committed a
serious error. He did not consult the priests and people of
the parish, who reacted vehemently to the donation—not so
much to the gift itself, but to the manner in which it was
accomplished. Under a lot of pressure, Sheen reversed his
decision. One priest commented: "If the bishop wants to
make some grand gesture, he could move in with the poor

and live among them. Then maybe he would be selling his books instead of giving away Church property." The incident again points to the ambiguity of the man and the contradictory quality of almost everything he did.

Sheen never recovered from this episode. Things would never be the same for him again in Rochester. However, he began many other changes. He put the diocesan finances under the control of a comptroller, saying, "The first thing I did was to put the diocese on a sound business basis. The Lord made a mistake once when he put a priest in charge of money." He revised the seminary training, appointing such diverse teachers as English-born Douglas Hyde, a one-time Communist who became a professor and taught the history of communism and the possibility of Christian-Marxist dialogue. Sheen had a Presbyterian minister instruct the future priests how to preach, which prompted one cleric to remark, "We are going to have a generation of priests giving Presbyterian sermons." Sheen appreciated the worth of a lay board whose purpose was to evaluate continuously the qualifications of candidates to the priesthood, observing, "In the past the parish accepted the priest sent to them by the bishops. Now the laity will have a voice in determining the type of priest to be sent."

Sheen raised the age of Confirmation to seventeen or eighteen so that the young would be old enough to make a commitment. He levied taxes on all Church construction, to be given to the poor. He ordered some home masses especially to be held in the homes of the poor. When Sheen celebrated one of those home masses himself, he did so with all the pomp of a prince. He sent an aide out to line up a poor black home. Sheen arrived like an oriental monarch, with his clerical entourage and several suitcases. He said the mass on the kitchen table in his ceremonial robes, including mitre and white gloves. On one such an occasion, when he departed, the black housewife summed up her feelings, "I never felt so rich, or so poor." To many of the poor, the Church appears as a luxurious jewelry store does to a destitute man looking through its windows. Sheen was never an appropriate choice for Rochester. A man once fitted to succeed Spellman was now listless and unhappy in his clerical Siberia. A friend of his commented, "After being on the heights of Mount Tabor all his life, the bishop found his calvary in Rochester."

Sheen tried desperately to be the American Pope John. But they were completely different men. Sheen is a pretentious man. The "Fat Christ," Pope John, affectionately dubbed Johnny Walker by the Romans because of his tours throughout the city, was sprung from farmer stock. He was in the best sense a true revolutionary; he was a reconciler. He was a modern man, a man for all seasons, someone who kept continuity with the past, yet he made his predecessors in the Twentieth Century seem like reactionaries. "The compatibility of Theology and science was to him a challenge for the Church in its efforts to understand a world in turmoil. John had a charismatic warmth and pliancy. He was a humble priest with no pretension, who loved people rather than ideas. Sheen is a many-faceted man, always on stage. Just after his election to the papacy, Pope John was besieged by requests from famous photographers anxious to make his portrait. Following one such episode, Sheen was ushered in for an audience. Pope John greeted the man from Peoria with these words, "The good Lord knew from all eternity I would become Pope—wouldn't you think he could have made me a little more photogenic?"

In Rochester Sheen never followed through on his ideas, many of which were brilliant. He urged people to write to him personally; they received form letters in reply. Discouraged in a forty-minute audience in May 1969, he pleaded with Pope Paul to be released from his Rochester post. Rochester was the last act of the Greek tragedy. When he arrived there he said, "He would like to get his arms around Rochester." He never succeeded in doing so. The people never returned the embrace. Many saw Sheen's appointment to Rochester as a demotion, as his being put out to pasture. Was he forced to resign the Rochester post, or did he see the writing on the wall and willingly step down? He denied Rochester was a clerical Siberia. He compared himself to an astronaut wanting a place of re-entry, a place to touch down. "For me, Rochester is that point, and a good one." His parachute for the re-entry never opened, and he fell flat on his face.

Sheen all his life needed a good public relations man. He never had one. He rarely handled the press properly and nowhere was this truer than in Rochester. A priest commented: "He wouldn't see them (the press)—he wouldn't answer their questions. He was not frank and honest when he met with them. After a while they began to dig him every chance they could."

Sheen has a superlatively quick mind, a supreme command of the English language and the spoken word—a well-nigh hypnotic power to captivate, inspire, persuade, and stimulate. On the other hand, there was within him a capability to belittle, antagonize, and alienate, which later led to his downfall.

On October 15, 1969, Sheen announced his surprise resignation, to a jammed press conference: "I'm resigning from the diocese, I am not resigning from work. I am preparing to regenerate." He was raised to the rank of archbishop and titular head of Newport, England, a diocese which no longer exists. On the "Merv Griffin Show," when the smiling former choirboy from California joked with him about being without a job and a Church, Sheen replied that all America was his Church.

Sheen revealed that on May 8, his seventy-fourth birthday, he had personally asked Pope Paul to allow him to resign. When the Holy Father asked him what date he hoped the retirement might begin, Sheen chose September 20—his fiftieth anniversary as a priest. Sheen added, "The Holy Father smiled. Wrote the date on a pad and put a question mark after it." When Sheen asked the reason for the question mark, the Pope replied, "Oh, it won't be long after that."

Newsmen pressed Sheen with the obvious question, "Will you please tell us why you asked the Pope for retirement at seventy-four? Wasn't this request a whole year in advance of the time you would have been obliged to submit the resignation?" Sheen: "No—I will not tell you. That reason is known only to the Holy Father." Thus ended the ambiguous thousand days.

Sheen's sojourn in Rochester was marked by discouragement, disappointment, and frustration. He told a newsman, "I have never had a happy day in Rochester." Sheen's problem was in the fact that he is an idea man, not an executive —a bishop has to be top. A bishop's office used to be looked up to. That day is over. Sheen said, "Today he is the sponge, the object of vulnerability, who must absorb the trials, crosses, protests, sufferings, and misunderstandings." Sheen has been a prophet in many ways—way ahead of his time. In a tear-jerking dramatic farewell to Rochester, Sheen twelve times asked forgiveness for all his failings. He said, "I was too young for the old persons, and too old for the young persons." If Sheen had been thirty years younger when he went to Rochester, he would have had the charisma, the class, and the ability to lead the American Church to a new frontier. But he is now out of the scheme of things; an old man in the evening of life—and we are without a captain. Nevertheless, we are grateful to have lived in the days of Sheen. Of one thing we can be sure— we shall never see his vintage again.

In another time, in another country, he would have been

either a king or a revolutionary, and he would have effected a lot of change. Yet he knows, like all of us, how much change you can effect when the establishment stifles you. He is a restless, frustrated man who was turned off by an institution he never really was part of, yet he never could leave. Fulton means war; Sheen means peace. Shalom, Fulton J. Sheen.

The lesson of his life is that there must be more freedom in the Church, men must be allowed to be themselves, to become more human and more free. Of the myriad lessons of Sheen's life, the one that stands out is that "You have not converted a man because you have silenced him."

EPILOGUE

RESURRECTION

THE LAST time I saw Archbishop Sheen was a cold Friday evening in New York City in October of 1970. I was having a wedding rehearsal in the Church of Sts. Faith, Hope, and Charity on Park Avenue. Into the church walked a man with a shock of gray hair and a newspaper in his overcoat pocket. The man was Sheen. He knelt down, bent his head in silent prayer, got up, looked around quickly and went out into the night, presumably on his way to his apartment on East Seventy-eighth Street. I recalled Dick Cavett quipping jocosely to Sheen on his TV show in January of 1970, "You are living in a bachelor apartment. Do you go to a Singles Club at night?"

Sheen again did an apparently contradictory thing which brought complaints from both liberal Christians and Jews. On the fourth of July 1970, he appeared in Washington, with Evangelist Billy Graham and Rabbi Marc Tanenbaum at the "Honor America Day" ceremonies engineered by the conservative supporters of the Nixon-Agnew policy. In view of his dovish approach to the Vietnam War, this appearance did not seem to be consistent with his policy.

Milton Berle once humorously remarked that when he and Sheen were scheduled to appear at the same hotel for a benefit, Sheen arrived in a Rolls Royce with stained-glass windows. On a Mike Douglas Show once, Douglas asked Sheen if he was camera shy and Milton Berle, his co-host, interjected, "Camera shy—why he is a bigger ham than I was!!" Sheen was a great performer, but there was a lot more to the man than that. He was the type of man around whom rumors and apocryphal tales flourished like bees around a honeycomb. There are few neutralists as far as Sheen was concerned: you were Sheenophile, all for him, or "agin him." This story has attempted to be neither a virulent hatchet job nor a work of sickening adulation. It tries to portray the real Sheen—certainly an extraordinary man.

Sheen was a player of many roles, a great man with many weaknesses. He found his calvary in Rochester but he himself once said that to have a faith greater than failure is the greatest of all victories. He apparently lost the battle—a victim of ecclesiastical politics—but he won the war: he preserved his own integrity, and that is what life is all about.

Many small men held big positions in the Catholic Church. Sheen was more intelligent than all of them. He was a giant of a man—a prophet ahead of his time. He deciphered the dangers of communism in the 1930's; he saw the risks of overreacting to it in the 1960's and in 1970. He was a poverty program all on his own before the phrase The Third World was ever coined. He was the religious miracle of the mass media—radio, TV, and press—an area in which his Church was never comfortable and which it never really used to its benefit.

On the Mike Douglas Show in October of 1970, the Philadelphia Kid posed this question to the man from Peoria, Fulton J. Sheen:

Douglas: "Would you like to be a young priest coming up today?"

Sheen: "No."

Douglas: "Why?"

Sheen: "Oh, the Lord has given me one chance and I've tried to do my best and I am anxious to be with Him."

Sheen's best was better than most.

INDEX